THE POLITICAL CONSEQUENCES OF
ELECTORAL LAWS

THE POLITICAL
CONSEQUENCES OF
ELECTORAL LAWS

Revised Edition

by
DOUGLAS W. RAE

NEW HAVEN AND LONDON
YALE UNIVERSITY PRESS

Published with assistance from the fund
established in memory of William McKean Brown.

Library of Congress catalog card number: 74–161209
ISBN: 0–300–01517–8 (cloth), 0–300–01518–6 (paper)

Designed by Marvin H. Simmons
and set in Janson type.
Printed in the United States of America by
The Carl Purington Rollins Printing-Office of the
Yale University Press, New Haven, Connecticut.

Distributed in Great Britain, Europe, and Africa by
Yale University Press, Ltd., London; in Canada by
McGill-Queen's University Press, Montreal; in Latin
America by Kaiman & Polon, Inc., New York City; in
Australasia by Australia and New Zealand Book Co.,
Pty., Ltd., Artarmon, New South Wales; in India by
UBS Publishers' Distributors Pvt., Ltd., Delhi; in
Japan by John Weatherhill, Inc., Tokyo.

FOR MY PARENTS
Reverend and Mrs. W. Douglas Rae

PREFACE TO THE REVISED EDITION

This revised edition includes a new chapter and two (forgive me) fresh appendixes. The new Chapter 10 tries to cope with the alleged connection between P.R., the multiplication of parties, and government instability. Its more theoretical, analytic strategy is quite alien to the doggedly inductive strategy of the original study, and no effort has been made to integrate the two. I have added the new chapter because the original study was not designed to answer its question, yet it is reasonable to expect a book with the present title to do so—especially if it is to find its way into the classroom. As for the appendixes, one gives country-by-country data for fractionalization and the other presents a summary of some district-level results on the payoff thresholds of various electoral formulae.

Even this small revision requires acknowledgments: for money, Yale University and the Guggenheim Foundation; for hospitality, the University of Essex, England; for help and criticism, John Loosemore, Vic Hanby, and Mike Taylor; for patience, my wife, Nat; and for persisting errors, myself or perhaps the over-gentle colleagues who reviewed the original edition.

D.W.R.

New Haven
May 1971

PREFACE

This study analyzes relationships between electoral laws and political party systems on a cross-national scale. Since these relationships are found in any political system with institutionalized, partisan elections—the liberal democracies —this cross-national strategy seems appropriate. Accordingly, I have tried to isolate those relationships between electoral laws and party systems which are general to the twenty liberal democracies included in the study, or to subclasses within the twenty. The emphasis is on the cross-national verification of certain hypothises, expressed as propositions in the text, and not on the description of events unique to individual national histories. These unique events are treated here only as specific instances of broad patterns.

This strategy has forced me to put aside an enormous array of specific behavioral and institutional nuances within individual nations and individual political parties. This deliberate exclusion is essential to the aim of the study— cross-national theory—but it does mean that no political system is described as fully as I would have liked, and unique events are often underplayed. Any complete knowledge of electoral politics would necessarily give a greater appreciation to the particular, the unique, and even the perverse in political behavior. But too often, I think, we give so much attention to these unique instances that the general pattern by which they are connected to each other escapes us. The aim of this particular study is the general, cross-national pattern; other studies will, I hope, take up the less general.

I trust that the general relationships analyzed here will be of some use to the scholar who is concerned with these specific instances. By knowing what is generally the case, we equip ourselves to identify events which are unusual, and which therefore require specific explanation. Perhaps this interplay between general patterns and specific variations will be helpful in the construction of general, empirically verified political theory.

With respect to long-run historical patterns—why does the United States have a two-party system?—I have avoided causal assertions. I believe that causal analysis of such complex events would require the interplay of this sort of cross-national analysis and a much fuller appreciation of other variables which are important to political history. The quirks of individual behavior, as they are conditioned by that which is unique to given national cultures, would need to be identified and included in any such causal explanation. And the underlying socioeconomic pattern within each society would need to be accounted for. Similarly, the developmental sequences of political events which constitute the national past of individual nations could not be ignored. None of this is offered by this study, and I am therefore compelled to resist the urge to crystallize any causal model at this point. If the present study makes any contribution to causal explanation, it may be largely in defining some of the patterns which require explanation.

Many people—in and out of professional political science —helped in the preparation of this book.

The book originated as a Ph.D. thesis, written at the University of Wisconsin under the guidance of Austin Ranney, who was a most patient and generous teacher. I am also grateful to a variety of other teachers, notably Charles Hyneman of Indiana University; Don McCrone, Jack Dennis, Rufus Browning, Herbert Jacob, Michael Aikin, and Charles Anderson, all of the University of Wisconsin; and Thomas and Sondra Thorson, of the University of Toronto. I also wish to thank a number of my colleagues at Syracuse University's Maxwell School—Wayne Francis, Fred Frohock, Mike O'Leary, Guthrie Birkhead, George Frederickson, Frank Munger and Steve Hartman—for their advice. And for her valuable editing, I thank Ruth L. Davis of Yale University Press.

I am also indebted to my family. My wife, Natalie, made life more fun than an author has any right to expect, and also helped with the compilation of data. My mother, Katherine, typed the original manuscript, and my father W. Douglas Rae, gave valuable assistance. My brother, Duncan, helped less directly.

I personally made the mistakes which remain.

D.W.R.

January 1967

CONTENTS

TABLES AND FIGURES

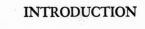

INTRODUCTION

CHAPTER 1

THE POLITICAL CONSEQUENCES OF ELECTORAL LAWS

The Problem

If the law were a matter of indifference to the groups whose interests are affected by it, then politics—the process by which law is formed—would be a matter of indifference to us all.[1] But the law and its administration vitally affect the interests of groups and their members. Any law has some consequences, whether good or ill, for all of the groups which enter the sphere of life to which it applies. Families, business corporations, churches, universities, interest associations, are all caught up in laws which condition their development, and ultimately influence their capacity to survive. Because the consequences of laws are important, politics is important.

This study is concerned with the political consequences of one especially important class of laws: those which govern the conduct of elections. These *electoral laws*[2] are of special importance for every group and individual in the society, because they help to decide who writes other laws. The groups whose interests are most directly affected by

1. "Law" is used here in a very general sense to include the whole of public policy.
2. See Chapter 2, below, for a definition of electoral laws.

electoral laws are, of course, *political parties*,[3] competing for the right to organize the legislative process for a nation and its people. How do electoral laws affect the interests of these parties? And, to generalize the question, how do electoral laws shape nations' political party systems? These are the questions to which I address this study.

A considerable body of theory has already accumulated in answer to these questions. Since free elections were first held, the men who conducted and contested them have been necessarily sensitive to the content of the electoral law. A century ago, when free general elections were young even in England, two of the most distinguished nineteenth-century political thinkers—John Stuart Mill and Walter Bagehot—disagreed polemically over the justice of the electoral law used to elect Parliament.[4] Their argument crystallized the issue which remains salient even today for every democratic government: should we adopt Anglo-American "first-past-the-post" electoral laws or some variety of "proportional representation"?[5] And, unfortunately, the polemical style of the Mill-Bagehot controversy is still characteristic of much of the literature on the question.

Perhaps its polemical sting explains the persistent, almost worldwide interest which has been generated by the argument over the political consequences of electoral laws. In the United States, E. E. Schattschneider, V. O. Key, and Leslie Lipson have joined the issue.[6] In France, Maurice Duverger and A. Dami have examined the party politics of

3. See Chapter 3 below for a description of political party systems.

4. John Stuart Mill, *Considerations on Representative Government* (London, Longmans, Green, 1890), and Walter Bagehot, *The English Constitution* (New York, D. Appleton, 1877).

5. These alternatives are detailed in Chapter 2 below.

6. E. E. Schattschneider, *Party Government* (New York, Holt, Rinehart and Winston, 1942); V. O. Key, Jr., *Politics, Parties and Pressure Groups* (5th ed. New York, Thomas Y. Crowell, 1964); and Leslie Lipson, "The Two-Party System in British Politics," *American Political Science Review*, 47 (June 1953), 337–58.

electoral laws.[7] In a more theoretical vein, George van den Bergh of the Netherlands and Giovanni Sartori of Italy have recently set out important, diametrically opposed positions on the justice and efficacy of electoral laws.[8] Wolfgang Birke of West Germany and James Hogan of Ireland have also added their thoughts to the literature.[9] In Great Britain, Enid Lakeman, James D. Lambert, William J. M. Mackenzie, and David E. Butler have offered a very heterogeneous collection of facts and opinions.[10] Indeed, it is probably safe to suppose that no liberal democracy is without its literature on electoral laws and their political consequences.

Despite the volume of this literature, present knowledge about the politics of electoral law is neither very general in scope nor entirely reliable in content. No general and precise propositions have been tested systematically against the recorded facts of electoral politics. A few excellent single-country studies, like David E. Butler's *The Electoral System in Britain Since 1918*, and Uwe Kitzinger's *German Electoral Politics* stand out as very systematic and reliable, yet undeniably particularized, commentaries.[11] More gen-

7. Maurice Duverger, *L'Influence des Systèmes Electoraux sur la Vie Politique* (Paris, Armand Colin, 1954); Maurice Duverger, *Political Parties* (New York, John Wiley and Sons, 1954); and A. Dami, *Science* "In Support of Proportional Representation," *International Social Bulletin, 3* (Summer 1951), 353–57.

8. George van den Bergh, *Unity in Diversity: A Systematic Critical Analysis of All Electoral Systems* (London, B. T. Batsford, 1956), and Giovanni Sartori, *Democratic Theory* (New York, Frederick A. Praeger, 1965).

9. Wolfgang Birke, *European Elections by Direct Suffrage* (Leyden, A. W. Sythoff, 1961), and James Hogan, *Elections and Representation* (University College, Cork, Cork University Press, 1945).

10. Enid Lakeman and James D. Lambert, *Voting in Democracies* (London, Faber and Faber, 1955); William J. M. Mackenzie, *Free Elections: An Elementary Textbook* (New York, Rinehart and Company, 1958); and David E. Butler, *The Electoral System in Britain Since 1918* (London, Oxford University Press, 1963).

11. Butler; and Uwe W. Kitzinger, *German Electoral Politics* (London,

eral, but less systematic comments are offered by Duverger's *L'Influence des Systèmes Electoraux sur la Vie Politique*, and *Voting in Democracies* by Lakeman and Lambert. The result is a conventional wisdom which provides many clues to general relationships, and careful analyses of particular ones, but which is more or less innocent of precise general knowledge.

The limitations of the existing literature reflect the three most persistent shortcomings of its component studies: (1) categories of analysis are seldom defined precisely, (2) data are almost never treated systematically, and (3) the standards of verification are usually left inexplicit. The properties of electoral laws—ballot forms, districts, "formulae"—are not classified according to explicit, precise categories, and party systems are usually described in similarly vague terms. Data are often confined to the experience of a single country, and, when many nations are treated comparatively, discomforting "exceptions" are often dismissed without modification of general assertions; the population of facts is either very small or, worse yet, undefined. Standards of evidence—what array of facts confirms or upsets a generalization?—are typically left flexible or even unstated, with the result that it is difficult to estimate the validity of many generalizations.

This assessment does not mean that the literature is without substantial merit; it means simply that no systematic and empirically verified body of knowledge yet exists for the political consequences of electoral law. If I were asked to predict the consequences of some alteration in an actual electoral law, it would be difficult or impossible to make a reliable deduction from this literature. One could repeat persuasive and insightful statements from the literature, but

Oxford University Press, 1960). See also J. F. S. Ross, *The Irish Election System* (London, Pall Mall Press, 1959); Arye Arazi, *Le Système Electoral Israelien* (Geneva, Librarie Droz, 1963); and Peter Campbell, *French Electoral Systems and Elections Since 1789* (London, Faber and Faber, 1958).

would certainly be unable to estimate the reliability of these statements. These are symptoms of a gap in our knowledge, and I have tried in this study to make a contribution toward filling it.

Approach and Organization

I have begun by formulating a series of "variables," which describe electoral laws and political party systems. I hope these have been formulated with enough precision that my analysis can be followed, or even reproduced, by the reader with no more information about them than I have written down. Chapter 2 sets out a classification of electoral laws, and shows how actual laws can be compared. Chapter 3 sets forth a number of variables which measure the main quantitative aspects of party competition. Together, these variables are meant to provide the categories of analysis used throughout the study.

Second, I have collected data for the outcomes of general legislative elections in twenty Western democracies: Australia, Austria, Belgium, Canada, Denmark, Finland, France, West Germany, Great Britain, Iceland, Ireland, Israel, Italy, Luxembourg, the Netherlands, New Zealand, Norway, Sweden, Switzerland, and the United States. These statistics cover elections held between January 1, 1945, and January 1, 1965—a twenty-year span. Two specific data have been collected for each party in each election: (1) the total number of popular votes its candidates obtained, and (2) the number of legislative seats it was awarded. The elections considered are those for the lower house (if there are two) of each nation's legislature or parliament.[12] These data constitute the population of facts by which I have tested my findings.

These are, of course, "aggregate data": they describe col-

12. A full list of the elections included, by nation and date, will be found in Appendix C.

lective events, not individual acts. I have chosen to use information of this kind instead of, say, sample survey data, for reasons best articulated by Austin Ranney:

> the availability and inexpensiveness of aggregate data invite replicative and comparative studies on a wide scale . . . [Aggregate election returns] . . . are the "hardest" data we can get, in the sense that their meaning and comparability vary less from area to area, from time to time, and from study to study than do most survey data. . . . Whatever complex socio-psychological processes may underlie the voter's decisions to make particular allocations, the votes themselves constitute a basic medium of political exchange. Thus their relative "hardness" as much as their accessibility, makes election returns a significant body of data for political analysis.[13]

The case for aggregate data is strengthened further by the fact that I am interested in aggregate events, and the behavior of individual candidates and voters need not be specified in order to understand the collective relationships in which I am interested.

Third, I have formulated my major findings in propositional form, wording them in terms which lead to empirical predictions which can in turn be tested against the data. Logically, these propositions approximate the form prescribed by Carl G. Hempel's "Requirement of complete falsifiability in principle," which suggests that, "A sentence has empirical meaning if and only if its denial is not analytic and follows from some finite logically consistent class of observation sentences." [14] For example, the proposition, "Plu-

13. Austin Ranney, "The Utility and Limitations of Aggregate Data in the Study of Electoral Behavior," *Essays on the Behavioral Study of Politics*, ed. Austin Ranney (Urbana, University of Illinois Press, 1962), p. 96.
14. Carl G. Hempel, "The Empiricist Criterion of Meaning," *Logical Positivism*, ed. A. J. Ayer (New York, The Free Press, 1959), p. 113.

rality electoral formulae cause two-party systems," is open to falsification by the observation that "Canada has a plurality electoral formula and a multi-party system." Only if a proposition is open to falsification by the available data and yet remains unfalsified, have I suggested its general validity. Ultimate "proof" is, of course, impossible under this test, or under any other scientifically accepted standard. Under this sort of standard, however, it is possible at least to show precisely how much evidence, of what kind, supports the generalization. As the reader will see, I have disregarded most of the involuted, sometimes silly rigors of the logical positivism which this standard of meaning might seem to imply. The standard is simply a "working guide" for the evaluation of hypotheses.

These three tactics—explicit variables, systematic data, and a consistent standard of verification—should yield a small corpus of general, precise, and reliable knowledge about the politics of electoral law. Hopefully, this body of knowledge will provide the "critical examination of common-sense notions concerning the working of political institutions and procedures" [15] which Carl J. Friedrich suggests is the main job of the political scientist.

15. Carl J. Friedrich, *Constitutional Government and Democracy* (Boston, Ginn and Co., 1941), pp. 593–94.

PART I
THE VARIABLES

CHAPTER 2

ELECTORAL LAWS

Comparing electoral laws on a cross-national scale is a little like trying to compare the flowers in a distant field. The flowers are at first indistinguishable from the ground around them; only by squinting to exclude irrelevant perceptions can they be set apart. And when the flowers are first seen as a distinct group, they seem identical with each other, devoid of perceptible variation in color, shape, or size. As one walks closer, broad classes can be distinguished; daisies are, for example, distinguished from dandelions. And if one walks into the field, looking at single flowers, it is suddenly apparent that no two of them are alike. Species are not altogether homogeneous; no two members share the same combination of tints, shapes, dimensions. One must find the properties that account for similarities and differences between individuals. So it is that we begin this chapter by asking how electoral laws differ from other kinds of law, and then by trying to specify the variables by which we may compare them across time and national boundaries.

Electoral Law Defined

How can we distinguish electoral laws from the broader class of laws which govern elections—"election laws"?

Electoral law may be defined *per genus et differentiam* against the background of this larger class of laws. If we agree that *laws* generally are authoritative rules of conduct enacted and enforced by the holders of governmental authority, than *election laws* are those authoritative rules which pertain to the conduct of elections.

Since elections are very complex institutions, the laws which regulate the conduct of participants in them will necessarily be multiple and multi-purposive. Laws of suffrage and eligibility will, for example, specify the classes of persons who may or may not participate as voters and candidates. Other laws will apportion seats and districts among provinces, regions, or population groups. From these and other varieties of election laws, it is necessary to distinguish the set relevant here, namely, *electoral law.*

Electoral laws are those which govern the processes by which electoral preferences are articulated as votes and by which these votes are translated into distributions of governmental authority (typically parliamentary seats) among the competing political parties. Are the voters asked to choose between men or parties? Does the candidate or party with more votes than any other win outright or is the victory divided among the contestants in proportion to their vote? Does the voter express a nominal preference—"this, not those"—or is he asked to rank his preferences among a number of alternatives? Does each district choose a single legislator, or does it select a number of them?

The answers to these questions are interdependent; an answer to any one limits the answers the law may reasonably give to the others. For example, single-member districting and elaborate rules for proportionality, at least at the district level, are incompatible. It is this interdependence which leads political scientists and politicians alike to regard the total pattern of electoral laws prevailing for a particular country's general elections as an organic whole—an "electoral system." [1] The study assumes that this total pattern can best be understood if it is first factored into its main components. If, instead, one classifies systems according to common "ideal types"—"majority systems" or "proportionality systems"—he finds that the exceptions which must be made are so numerous and so important that nothing very useful can be said. A cross-national analysis of electoral systems resting on these "ideal types" might well read like the proverbial textbook on comparative anatomy which begins, "Elephants and butterflies can both fly, except for the elephants."

Despite the interdependence of electoral laws in any given system, cross-national variation is so great that it demands recognition in the form of a systematic classification based on explicit institutional variables. These variables describe the provisions which *any* electoral system must possess, and then elaborate the ranges and types of variation which may appear in the particular provisions of actual electoral systems.

Electoral Law Variables

A word of warning is required: the variables which follow do not provide a complete description of electoral laws in all their aspects, since they are meant to focus our attention on only those aspects of electoral systems which have important ramifications for interparty competition. If this were an anlysis of *intra*party politics—organization, cohesion, decision-making—a very different series of variables would be used. For example, a variable for ballot structure would draw attention to candidate-party relations instead of party-party relations. And if this were a general treatise

1. It should be clear that we are analyzing *laws* in this study: electoral systems are compounded of laws. We will use the terms interchangeably but it must be understood that the word "system" is used idiomatically.

on electoral law, both variables would be needed. In brief, these variables are designed for this particular study, and sensitize us to only those electoral provisions with the clearest implications for interparty competition.

The working of an electoral system may be conveniently divided into three phases, each of which is an important source of variation: (1) balloting as a specification of the voter's role in deciding the election, (2) districting as a limiting factor in the translation of votes to seats, and (3) electoral formulae as key factors in the translation of votes to seats. Since all three phases are sources of variation, each requires a device for the measurement of variation. In what follows, variables are constructed for each of them.[2]

The Ballot and the Voter's Role: Categorical and Ordinal Choices

During an election campaign the voter plays out an essentially passive role, unless he is also a campaign activist. During this period he is bombarded with the rival appeals of the contestants, each urging him to decide in its favor on election day. When the day arrives, the voter's role is suddenly, albeit temporarily, reversed; he is now expected to act positively, to make a choice. And, taken collectively, the decisions made by the voters in a general election become the crucial force upon which the entire process turns.[3] In democratic elections, voting is necessarily an act of choice.

The function of the ballot is to structure that choice: to specify the role of the voter. All ballots ask the voter to choose among the contestants in some way, but they vary in the kind of choice they demand. The general election bal-

2. A further limitation should be noted: the variables are, in principle, universal, but I have demonstrated their application only to systems actually used in one or more of the elections studied. The number of systems in print but not in use is an astounding testament to the reach of man's political imagination.

3. See Proposition Six, Chapter 4, below.

lots analyzed in this study demand two fundamentally different choices, which differ most critically in the degree to which they require a categorical choice. The variable, which we shall call ballot structure, has two "stops": (1) *categorical* ballots, and (2) *ordinal* ballots.

Categorical ballots ask the voter to decide which one of the parties he prefers. The ballot forces him to say that he prefers *one* party in parliament as opposed to *all* others. He cannot equivocate; he cannot qualify his decision. In some cases he can give qualified references among the candidates of a single party, but he cannot divide his mandate among parties or among candidates of different parties. The *simple candidate ballots* used in British, most Commonwealth, American, and recent French elections are important illustrations of categorical balloting.[4] *Simple party-list ballots*, used in many European systems, are also categorical, since they allow no interparty division of a single elector's mandate. Whether or not these list ballots allow intercandidate choice (as they do in Norway, for example), the essential point for interparty competition is that a voter must choose a single party as the recipient of his mandate. The mathematically minded reader may prefer to call categorical ballots "nominal," since they insist that the voter express himself at only this rude level. The term categorical is used here to suggest the unequivocal quality of the decision which is required.

By way of contrast, ordinal ballots allow the voter to express a more complex, equivocal preference by rank-ordering the parties. He may thus say that he prefers Party A most, Party C second, and so forth. The voter need not opt in favor of any single contestant. An example of the ordinal ballot is the *alternative candidate ballot* used in Australia for the federal House of Representatives and in Ireland's

4. Under these ballots, the voter must choose categorically among candidates for any one legislature. These candidates may or may not carry party labels.

application of the Hare system, which asks the voter to rank his preferences among the candidates of different parties. The *cumulative party-list ballot* illustrates a variation of the principle by allowing each voter to distribute his numerous mandates among party lists in proportions of his own choosing. *Panachage party-list ballots* also produce an ordinal effect by allowing the voter to award single mandates to candidates appearing on various party lists.[5] Under ordinal ballot systems, the voter is not compelled to decide unequivocally in favor of a single party. He may instead distribute his mandate among a number of competing parties.

The significant difference between these two types of ballot lies in the nature of the role imposed by each upon the voter. Under categorical systems the voter must act decisively, delivering his whole mandate to a single party. Under ordinal systems the voter is not required to act quite so decisively, and is allowed to represent even his least powerful positive feelings in small parcels of support for each of several parties. In the microcosm of the single voter's behavior, categorical systems are distinguished from ordinal systems by their intractable rejection of compromise solutions. But what significance has this distinction for the macrocosm of the party system?

In this larger perspective, the major difference is that categorical systems channel each parcel of electoral strength into the grasp of a single party, while ordinal balloting may disperse each parcel of electoral strength among a number of competing parties. Categorical balloting, in fine, concentrates each micro-parcel of strength in a single receptacle, but ordinal systems impose no equivalent condensation of electoral success. If this difference is repeated for every member of the electorate, and other factors remain con-

5. *Panachage* is a system of voting which lets the voter choose a number of candidates without regard to the party lists on which their names appear.

stant, we would expect the categorical system to concentrate strength in fewer parties, while ordinal systems diffused it among a larger number of parties. As we will see, "other factors" are seldom constant.

The Magnitudes of Electoral Districts[6]

Electoral districts are the units within which voting returns are translated into distributions of parliamentary seats. These districts are usually defined territorially, but may also be defined by population groups, as are New Zealand's four Maori districts.[7] Electoral districts should not be confused with voting districts like the familiar American precinct, in which no allocation of seats takes place but in which voting returns are collected. The defining property of electoral districts is the fact that they are the units within which vote totals are translated into distribution of seats. In some cases, only a single seat is awarded in such a district, while in most of the districts examined in this study more than one seat is awarded.

This brings us to the well-known distinction between "single-member districts" and "multi-member districts." It is also an appropriate occasion to remind ourselves that multi-member districts may have as few as two seats each, but may also have upward of a hundred seats.[8] The underlying dimension here is neither geographic area nor population; it is the number of seats assigned to the district. This variable may be called the *magnitude* of the district, and is defined as the number of seats assigned by the electoral law to any district. Since fractional seats do not exist, district magnitudes vary as positive integers, ranging upward from a lower limit of one.

6. This refers to what Stein Rokkan calls the "unit of aggregation." See Stein Rokkan, "Electoral Systems," draft article.

7. *New Zealand Official Year Book, 1961* (Wellington, Government Printer, 1961), pp. 37, 1124.

8. The Netherlands and Israel offer such extreme cases.

Operationally, magnitude will be measured by the arithmetic mean of district magnitudes under any given electoral system. This mean is figured by dividing total seats by total districts. If (M) represents this mean magnitude, (X) stands for total seats, and (Y) for total districts, this computation may be expressed:

$$M = \frac{X}{Y} \; ^9$$

This procedure does not alert our analysis to interdistrict variation, but it does sensitize it to the general order of district magnitude which must be taken into account. Unlike individual district magnitudes, these average values will vary continuously over the fractional spaces between integers. Average magnitudes form an interval scale, making most statistical operations useful in their analysis.

It is necessary to take notice of some difficulties raised by actual electoral systems. No real difficulty occurs when a country is divided into any number of mutually exclusive districts, as is the case in Great Britain, the United States, and many other nations. And nations which have only one, all-inclusive district, such as Israel, are not troublesome.[10] However, systems that provide two tiers of districts, each covering the same space and population, raise some problems for the concept of district magnitude. If a second, superimposed layer of districts is not operative in the apportionment of seats, as is true of the "electoral circles," or *krieskringen* of the Dutch system, the difficulty is more apparent than real.[11] Each of the three laws adopted for West German elections since 1949, however, include two operative tiers of electoral districts—single-member constituencies plus

9. Capital letters always refer to national scale measures; small letters refer to district measures.

10. See Arazi, *Le Système Electoral Israelien.*

11. van den Bergh, *Unity in Diversity*, p. 36, and Robert C. Bone, "The Dynamics of Dutch Politics," *Journal of Politics, 24* (1962), 30.

either the *länder* or the nation.[12] This problem is tentatively resolved simply by counting the total number of districts at both levels in the computation of average magnitudes.[13] These two-tiered district systems are called "complex" in later discussions.

The importance of district magnitudes for the relationship between electoral law and party system hinges upon the "proportionality" of the electoral system—the degree to which each party's share of the votes is equaled by its share of the seats. W. J. M. Mackenzie suggests that, "The larger the number of seats in the constituency the more exact is the proportionality that can be attained." [14] Now, if it is also true that most disproportions in the allocation of seats advantage large parties and disadvantage small parties, then small district magnitudes will tend to concentrate seats in the already strong parties.[15] And large district magnitudes will not have that concentrating effect, leaving the seats relatively dispersed among smaller parties. Whatever the electoral formula, district magnitude will exert an influence. This set of expectations must await exact formulation after party system variables have been defined. Only then can empirical evidence be introduced.

Electoral Formulae

The electoral process ends with the distribution of parliamentary seats among the winning parties. But who has

12. Kitzinger, *German Electoral Politics,* pp. 17–37, and James K. Pollock, "The West German Electoral Law of 1953," *American Political Science Review,* 49 (1955), 107–30.

13. This applies only to district magnitudes, not allocative formulae. In this latter regard, the German systems are also difficult. The complexity of the German systems is not to be blamed on German thoroughness alone, since it was copied from an earlier Danish system.

14. Mackenzie, *Free Elections,* p. 61. See also Rokkan, "Electoral Systems," pp. 23–24. Rokkan suggests that the larger the magnitude of the district, the lower is the threshold at which parties win their first seats.

15. See Proposition One, Chapter 4, below, for confirmation of this assertion.

won? Which are the winning parties? How is it decided that a party with some number of votes is entitled to some other number of seats? How is victory distinguished from defeat? What, in fine, is the formula of victory?

In every electoral district, during every general election, these questions demand to be answered, and a significant part of any electoral law is given over to answering them. Unfortunately for the simplicity of this analysis, the electoral formulae which result are the source of enormous cross-national variation, and many of them are extremely complex.[16] Since balloting and districting have already been examined, it will be possible to limit the present discussion to the formulae as they apply in any one district, putting aside the problems of ballot structure and district magnitude for the moment. Indeed, it would defeat the analytic strategy I have been following to confuse these questions at this point. The discussion of electoral formulae can be simplified further, without losing any relevant information, if it is focused on the allocation of seats among parties, neglecting competition among the candidates of any single party, since this study is concerned primarily with the relationship between electoral laws and interparty competition.

Elections are artifacts of large-scale democracy, in which many electors must be represented by a few members of parliament. Voting returns are quantitative indices of the electorate's preferences among the minorities (parties) who seek to represent it. Within each electoral district, *the function of the electoral formula is to interpret these numerical data as the basis for a legitimate distribution of parliamentary seats among the competing parties.* The key issue in the construction of electoral formulae is therefore a quanti-

16. No really comprehensive treatment of electoral formulae has been published. The closest approximations are found in van den Bergh, *Unity in Diversity;* Lakeman and Lambert, *Voting in Democracies;* and Hogan, *Elections and Representation.*

tative one: *how many votes constitute a legitimate claim on each parliamentary seat?* Any attempt to discuss electoral formulae without benefit of agreement on a few algebraic terms is doomed to failure; the following terms will be used here:

- (v) the total vote returned in any district
- (t) any single party's share of the total vote (v)
- (m) the total seats assigned to any district (its magnitude)
- (s) any single party's share of the total seats (m)

There are three general sorts of answers to the issue at hand and there are, accordingly, three main kinds of electoral formulae: (1) majoritarian types, (2) plurality types, and (3) proportional representation (P.R.) types. Each of these is distinguished by its definition of a legitimate claim to any seat: majorities, pluralities, and proportionate shares. Each is examined below.

THE MAJORITY FORMULA

A majority exists when a single party has obtained more votes than its combined opposition. A majority is usually defined as one more than half the votes:

$$t = \frac{v}{2} + 1$$

Actually, this formulation is correct only if the total vote (v) is an even number; if the total is odd, the increase over half is not one, but one half. The minimum majority for five votes is three, only one-half integer above the half ($2\frac{1}{2}$). George van den Bergh suggests that the absolute majority "is half the number of valid votes, increased to the next integer." [17] Hence, a majority vote total may be defined:

$$t > \frac{v}{2} \text{ or } t = \frac{v}{2} + \ldots$$

17. van den Bergh, p. 92.

These formulae correspond to actual practice, while the simpler "plus one" formula does not. The essential point about the rule of majorities is that the winning party has defeated the entire field of opposition; no combination of opponents can match its numerical strength.[18] If Party A has a majority, then:

$$t_a > (t_b + t_c + t_d + \ldots t_n)$$

Despite its outward decisiveness, the majority system is seldom used in elections, although it is a common device in parliamentary decision-making itself. Of the twenty nations studied here, only two use the majority formula and neither application is unalloyed. Recent elections to the French National Assembly have been held under the "double-ballot" system familiar during the Third Republic. Under this system, election on the first ballot, but not on the second, requires an absolute majority.[19] Very few candidates obtain the required initial majorities, so they are elected on the second (plurality) ballot. Elections to the Australian House of Representatives are conducted entirely on a majority formula, under the alternative candidate ballot system.[20] If first preferences fail to produce a majority, the second preferences of the weakest candidate (who is eliminated) are divided among the others, and so forth, until a majority is established for one contestant.[21] This is not, of course, the exact equivalent of majority rule, since votes are not to be equated with voters. Although the United States does not use the majority rule in Congressional elections, the rule is applied to some primary elections in this country.

18. This accounts for the confinement of majority formulae to single-member districts. Higher magnitudes would complicate this simple concept beyond recognition.

19. Campbell, *French Electoral Systems*, pp. 134–35.

20. Joan Rydon, "Electoral Methods and the Australian Party System: 1901–1951," *The Australian Journal of Politics and History*, 2 (1956), 68–83, and Leslie F. F. Crisp, *The Parliamentary Government of the Commonwealth of Australia* (London, Longmans, 1961), pp. 66–68.

21. Lakeman and Lambert, pp. 54–56.

So we may conclude that the majority formula is rarely used in general parliamentary elections, and is never used without first being coupled with some other device to soften its harsh demands. This rarity is not brought about by the "disproportionality" of the majority formula; indeed it is more likely than the plurality formula to produce proportionate results. Rather, the majority formula is rare in elections largely because of its built-in propensity to produce deadlocks in which *no* party can win a given seat. Applied to legislation, this possibility of deadlock is absent, since a non-majority resolves whatever issue is at hand. But the possibility of electoral deadlock is so threatening to the viability of legislative institutions that majority elections are usually avoided.

This leads to the ironic conjecture that pure majority elections, which small parties cannot possibly win, may do more to encourage the genesis of splinter parties than even extreme systems of proportional representation. This is so because the possibility of deadlock carries with it the further possibility that any of several small minorities could obtain negative control of the situation by threatening to prevent *any* resolution of the election. If two parties could obtain a combined total of 90 per cent, yet neither could muster a majority, then smaller parties attracting a total of 10 per cent would enjoy a very strong bargaining position vis-à-vis either of the stronger competitors. So long as the two large parties were unwilling to cooperate, the small parties would enjoy at least as much control of the situation as either of them. Pure majority rule may, in brief, produce perversely unmajoritarian electoral politics.

THE PLURALITY FORMULA

A plurality exists when a single party has obtained more votes than its strongest single competitor, but has not necessarily polled a higher total than the combined opposition. Hence, the exact relationship between the plurality and the total vote defies a priori definition. The plurality is based instead on the relationships between actual party totals. Party A has a plurality where:

$$t_a > t_b$$
$$t_a > t_c$$
$$t_a > t_d$$
$$\cdots\cdots$$
$$t_a > t_n$$

It is this property which accounts for terms like "relative majority," and "first-past-the-post." The plurality formula makes an election a contest in which the object is to out-score the best of the opposition. Victory in interparty competition is all that matters. This, of course, introduces an element of "chance," since the number of votes required to win cannot be predicted from the formula and the vote total alone. The use of the plurality formula in four English-speaking nations—Great Britain, Canada, the United States, and New Zealand—obviously puzzles many European commentators. George van den Bergh is among them:

England is insular. It has manners and customs which differ in many respects from those of other countries. . . . There is hardly any international custom without England differing from it—even to the manner of scoring games of chess. . . . It is a strange experience —for us—when someone with 35 votes is elected chair-man, while two opponents get 25 and 30 votes respectively. But an Englishman, generally speaking, does not see anything uncommon in this. The first-past-the post system has struck root there. Does this expression perhaps denote that the system is bound up with the sporting spirit so inherent in this great nation? For a horse which is first to pass the winning post it is, indeed, a matter of indifference whether it has left one or many horses behind. It is the idol of the people—the many "also rans" only enhance its glory. Thus, the average Englishman considers the chairman with his 35 votes a smart fellow: he has left two opponents behind him, the one at a distance of 5, the other at a distance of 10 votes![22]

The point, in plurality elections, is to decide what single party has *won*, just as the object of racing is to decide which horse or automobile has traveled the distance most rapidly. Under the test of proportionality, plurality systems come off very badly; they produce greater disproportions than majority or P.R. systems under almost any circumstances. Indeed, it is generally believed that single-member plurality elections produce disproportions of cubic proportions.[23] That is, the ratio of seats between two parties approximates the cubed ratio of their votes:

$$\frac{S_a}{S_b} = \frac{T_a^3}{T_b^3}$$

In effect, the plurality system can reward strong parties out of all proportion to the size of their margins by giving the same reward to parties with 1 per cent margins as to those with 50 per cent margins. Hence, strong parties with support evenly spread over many districts may win a preponderant majority of the seats with fewer than half the total votes.

This suggests another difficulty in plurality formulae: the votes a party obtains beyond the minimum requirement are, in a sense, wasted.[24] It makes no difference that a party wins by a landslide in a district; a hair's breadth margin would do as well. I, personally, cannot accept the extreme rationalism

22. van den Bergh, p. 48.
23. M. G. Kendall and A. Stuart, "Cubic Proportion in Electoral Results," *British Journal of Sociology, 1* (1950), 183 ff. James G. March, "Party Legislative Representation as a Function of Election Results," *Public Opinion Quarterly, 21* (Winter 1957–58), 521–42.
24. In the same logic, the votes given losing candidates are also wasted.

which underlies this complaint, but in this I am no doubt the captive of my own Anglo-American culture. This difficulty, and the problem of proportionality generally, will be examined at greater length later on.

PROPORTIONAL REPRESENTATION FORMULAE

The principle of proportional representation is quite simple: the share of seats awarded to any party (s) should be equal to the share of the vote which it has won (t). This is the principle of "proportionate shares," and it is defined by the condition:

$$s = t$$

Or, in ratio:

$$\frac{s}{t} = 1$$

If, for example, a party has obtained 20 per cent of the total vote, it is properly awarded no more nor less than 20 per cent of the seats. And the same equality of shares must obtain for all parties within the electoral district at hand.

This stringent condition can be actualized only if each parliamentary seat "costs" the party to which it is awarded an exact and constant number of votes. For any district with (m) number of seats and (v) total votes, this constant cost (c) must be:

$$c = \frac{v}{m}$$

If this cost never varies from the prescribed value, then the equal shares condition (s = t) will necessarily be fulfilled. Each party, no matter what its share of the vote, will be assigned exactly that same share of the seats. An example of this "perfect" result is plotted in Figure 2.1 below. The values of (s) and (t) vary in exact proportion to each other; the performance of any party at the polls is a perfect predictor of the number of seats which will be awarded to it.

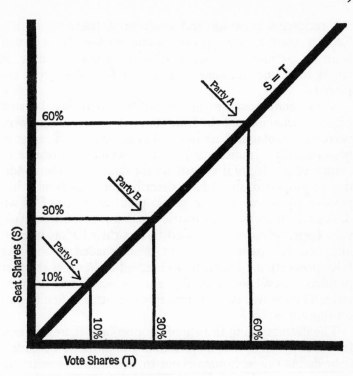

Figure 2.1
THE HYPOTHETICAL CONDITION OF PERFECT
PROPORTIONALITY

So far, I have been describing an idealized and perfectly symmetrical state of affairs. It is composed of fictitious conditions unrealized in the operation of any electoral formula the world has known. It is like a Platonic form, a model which real things resemble in various degrees but which is never duplicated in reality. It is the defining limit around which proportional representation formulae arrange themselves. For the proponents of P.R., these conditions amount to an algebraic outline of the *just* electoral order in which parties (and therefore their supporters in the electorate) are the recipients of exact and uniform distributive justice. Each receives his due, no more and no less. Later I will want to comment on this normative model; for now, it serves to define the class of electoral formulae being explored.

These conditions are never fulfilled in reality because political behavior and the institutions it produces are never perfectly regular and are not malleable enough to recast in geometrically symmetrical molds. It would be possible to construct an electoral system which duplicated the condition of proportionality I have described; it is apparently impossible to impose it upon actual political systems.[25] Two difficulties intervene: (1) district magnitudes must be made very large, or voters persuaded to cast their ballots in even lots, and (2) parliaments must be persuaded to institute fully proportional formulae. I observed earlier that the first problem is never solved totally, and the actual formulae examined below will demonstrate that the latter difficulty also remains unresolved.

The distinguishing feature of proportional representation formulae is that, unlike majoritarian and plurality formulae, they define the legitimate claim to parliamentary seats by the proportionality of shares. To win a seat, a party must win a number of votes proportionate to the seat's value. It need not, however, win a majority or plurality of the district's vote. And this formulation is qualitatively distinct from the others. The following paragraphs define the principal variations of the "proportionate shares" concept. Only formulae found in actual practice are included.

All of the actual formulae are computed from fractions similar to the "constant cost" ratio (v/m) mentioned earlier, but they differ from it and from each other in two respects. First, the values inserted in the cost fraction itself vary appreciably between formulae. Second, the arithmetic pro-

25. Israel, Denmark, Iceland, and the Netherlands approach this limit more closely than any other systems, but still fall short of it.

cedures in which these fractions are embedded differ from each other; the three leading alternatives are "highest average," "largest remainder," and "vote transfer." Considering these two sources of variation, it will be possible to define the four main variants of the proportional representation formula, each of which is applied somewhere within the twenty nations examined.

d'Hondt highest average formula. The term "average" refers to the ratio of votes to seats (t/s) for any party. It amounts to the average "cost" of each seat held by the party under examination. Under highest average formulae, the number of seats already held by a party, plus one, is the denominator of a fraction whose numerator is the party's total vote:

$$\frac{t}{s+1} = \text{"average"}$$

The seats in a district are formally awarded one at a time, new "averages" being computed for each party before each seat is allocated.[26] At any juncture, the party having the highest average is given the next seat. Since no party has any seats at the beginning of this procedure, the first denominator will be one (1.0) for each party. After a given party has won a seat, its denominator at the next stage will become two (2.0), while the "losing" parties retain the original denominators (1.0). By extension, the denominators come to vary with the sucess of a party, so that its effective strength declines proportionately.

However, unless district magnitudes are very great, the highest average procedure will handicap smaller parties. Each party will, at the end, have a "remainder," a residue of unused strength. For a smaller party which has won fewer seats (or none at all), this residue will be a higher proportion of its total and will therefore be more costly to it. For larger parties, which will have obtained more seats,

26. In practice, the computations are usually made simultaneously.

this remainder is proportionately less important; the average "cost" of its seats will be lower. This disproportionality is built into the highest average procedure itself.

If the "natural" numbers — 1, 2, 3 ... —are used in the denominator, these disproportions will be minimized. This is the simplest version of the highest average procedure, and is named for its inventor, Victor d'Hondt.[27] It is defined by the fraction cited above:

$$\frac{t}{s + 1} = \text{``average''}$$

Operationally, the denominator may be expanded to the series of numbers originally suggested by d'Hondt:

$$\frac{t}{1, 2, 3, 4 \ldots m}$$

Under the d'Hondt formula, the only disproportions introduced derive from the highest averages procedure, since the "natural" denominator series adds no handicap for the smaller parties, and no bonus for the larger parties. Needless to say, it offers no bonus to smaller parties, and no handicap to large ones. The fraction is, in short, a proportional one, while the procedure in which it is embedded is somewhat disproportional.

The minimum vote required to win *a* seat under this formula, and all other P.R. formulae, is a function of district magnitude and the degree to which the party system is fractionalized (i.e. the number of effective competitors). It will also vary with the total vote (v). According to Stein Rokkan, this minimum will vary according to the formula:

$$\text{Threshold} = \frac{\text{vote (v)} - 1}{\text{seats (m)} + \text{number of parties (n)} - 1} \quad [28]$$

27. Identical results may be obtained under the "Hagenbach-Bischoff formula" used in Austria. See Birke, *European Elections*, p. 62.
28. Rokkan, "Electoral Systems," p. 24.

It seems to me that the number of parties is alone inadequate; we need also to know their relative equality in votes. A party with a nil vote total (t) should not be equated with a very strong party, but this formula suggests the general shape of the relationship. The d'Hondt formula will therefore penalize small parties in the extreme unless the district magnitude is very large or the party system is highly fractionalized (see Chapter 3).

The moderately disproportional formula which results is found, for at least short periods, in eight of the systems studied: Austria, Belgium (where it was invented), Denmark (lower tier of districts), Finland, France (before 1958), West Germany, Norway (before 1953), and Switzerland (see Table 2.1 below).

Lague highest average formula. If, at a given level of district magnitude, the d'Hondt procedure fails to produce the desired effect, it may be altered by changing the series of denominators used in the averaging fraction. Such a modification apears in the Lague version of the highest average formula, in which the denominator used at each stage is inflated as follows:

Lague Denominators: 1.4   3.0   5.0   7.0 ... (2m — 1)
d'Hondt Denominators: 1.0   2.0   3.0   4.0 ... (m)

The Lague denominator series differs from the d'Hondt counterpart in two ways: (1) the first denominator is larger by 40 per cent, and (2) the relative distances between the members of the series are larger. This latter difference can be seen from the case of the distance between the second and third denominators:

Lague: 3 to 5. (5–3 = 2) relative distance = 2/5 = 0.40
d'Hondt: 2 to 3. (3–2 = 1) relative distance = 1/3 = 0.33

This differential holds throughout the sequence.

The effect of these alterations is suggested by Stein Rokkan as follows:

In its typical Scandinavian situation [the Lague formula] had a three-fold effect: it strengthened the middle-sized non-socialist parties by reducing the over-representation of the Social Democrats, . . . it reduced the pay-offs of mergers within the opposition, and it finally helped all the established parties by discouraging splinters and new parties.[29]

The formula seems then to advantage middle-sized parties by lowering the advantage obtained under all highest average procedures by the largest party, and by raising the threshold at which small parties begin to win seats. The limitation of big-party advantage appears to flow from the progressively higher cost of seats produced by the Lague denominator series. And the suppression of small party representation follows from the higher cost of the initial seat (1.4 units instead of 1.0 units).

The Lague formula is used presently in Norway, Sweden, and (in part) in Denmark.

Largest remainder formula. The largest remainder procedure begins with the computation of a "quota," which serves as the initial "price" for each seat. Ordinarily, this price is identical with the constant cost discussed earlier:

$$(q) \text{ or quota} = \frac{v}{m}$$

The Italians employ a variant intended to lower the price of the initial seats, helping weak parties.[30] Called the *"imperiali* largest remainder formula," this fraction is computed:

$$(q) = \frac{v}{m + 2}$$

29. Ibid., p. 18.
30. This is so only for the lower house. Here and elsewhere, I am discussing the electoral systems used for lower house elections, unless I specifically mention another legislature.

In either event, the quota will be used as the price of each seat; it will tell the officials in charge how many votes must be deducted from each party's vote (t) for every seat it is awarded. Initially, each party is given as many seats as its vote total contains the quota (q). This is established by division:

$$\text{Initial Allocation (s)} = \frac{t}{q}$$

For every whole integer in the resulting quotient, the party is awarded one seat. If all the seats in a district (m) are allocated at this point, the procedure has done its job. Since this is unlikely, provision is made for allocating the leftover seats to the parties with the *largest remainders* of votes, after one quota has been subtracted from each party's vote for each seat it has been given. These remainders may be computed:

$$\text{Remainder} = t - [(s)\,(q)]$$

The first "leftover" seat is awarded to the party with the largest remainder; the second to the party with the second largest remainder, and so forth, until the supply of seats is exhausted. Unless the *imperiali* fraction is used to establish the quota, the largest remainder formula is likely to produce more nearly proportional results than those produced by highest average formulae. This is because the usual wastage of unused remainders imposed on smaller parties will quite often be "paid back" by the largest remainder formula.[31] Small parties are therefore more likely to get a proportionate share of the seats under largest remainder formulae than under highest average formulae. This assumes, of course, that district magnitudes are constant, as is not often

31. The smaller parties also benefit because the threshold at which a first seat is won is lowered by the formula. Rokkan (ibid., p. 19) suggests that the threshold becomes:

$$\frac{v}{(m)\ (\text{number of parties})}$$

the case. Fairly small differences in district magnitudes are likely to erase these differences in formulae.

Largest remainder formulae are found in Denmark (for forty pooled seats only), provincial French districts (1951–57), Israel (after 1951), Italy (*imperiali* variation), and in Luxembourg (see Table 2.1).

Hare single transferable vote formula. Each of the P.R. formulae discussed above assumes that party-list ballots (with or without cumulation and *panachage*) have been used; the Hare formula assumes instead that alternative candidate ballots have been used. Since it attempts to account for rank-ordered preferences on each ballot paper, without "wasting" any first preferences, the Hare formula is complex. Actually, the formula described here—and used only for elections to the Irish Dail—is not identical with Thomas Hare's original prescription.[32] This Irish version has been buffed and polished to a high gloss of logical consistency, at the expense of intelligibility to the ordinary voter and the uninitiated student of politics. In approximately chronological order, here are the major stages of the procedure:

1. The ballot papers are sorted and counted according to first preferences.

2. Candidates having obtained one "Droop quota" in first preferences are declared elected. The Droop quota is computed:

$$\text{Droop quota} = \frac{v}{m+1}$$

3. The ballots of candidates so elected are sorted and counted according to second preferences. These are awarded to the unelected candidates receiving the second preferences in proportion to the "surplus" of the elected

32. Mill, *Representative Government*, pp. 53–65, offers the best easily available explanation of Hare's system.

candidate's totals. The second preferences are accordingly multiplied by the product of the formula:

$$\frac{\text{total vote for elected candidate} - \text{Droop quota}}{\text{total vote for elected candidate}}$$

which equals:

$$\frac{\text{elected candidate ``surplus''}}{\text{total vote for elected candidate}}$$

The vote awarded to another candidate at this point is figured:

$$\left(\frac{\text{elected candidate ``surplus''}}{\text{total vote for elected candidate}} \right) \times \left(\begin{array}{c} \text{second preferences} \\ \text{for the unelected} \\ \text{candidate} \end{array} \right)$$

4. Candidates now holding a Droop quota are declared elected. The candidate with the fewest votes is declared defeated, and his ballots are sorted and counted according to second preferences. These second preferences are distributed among the more fortunate yet unelected candidates. They are not "discounted."

5. Candidates now having a Droop quota are declared elected. Their ballots, and those of candidates declared elected at stage four, are sorted and counted for lower (second and third) preferences. These are awarded, at the discount outlined under stage three above, to remaining candidates.

6. This cyclic process is extended to lower and lower preference levels until all of the district's seats have been filled. In practice, the relatively low magnitude of Irish districts ($M = 3.7$) means that lower preferences will seldom be used.[33]

33. The best short description is found in Mackenzie, *Free Elections*, pp. 62–69. I have relied heavily upon it.

For computational purposes, the party affiliations of the candidates make no difference. It is not quite clear how this arrangement is likely to compare with other P.R. formulae as regards proportionality and party competition. Since only one case, the Irish, is available for analysis, and since district magnitudes there are quite small as P.R. systems go, it will not be possible to make precise comparisons with other formulae. For most purposes, I will treat the Irish formula as a case of P.R., without analyzing its unique properties in detail.

Combination formulae. Electoral systems with complex districting (i.e. two tiers of districts in the same area) make it possible to combine two formulae, one at each level. Denmark, for example, uses a Lague formula of highest averages at the lower level (for 135 seats), and a largest remainder formula for the upper level (40 seats). Cases of this kind must be examined individually, with special attention to the exact articulation between the tiers of districts, if their internal dynamics are to be understood completely. For many comparative purposes, however, it will be more useful to simply consider them P.R. formulae in a general sense.

I have been emphasizing the differences between the four main types of P.R. formula. For the purpose of clarity, this is probably the best procedure. But, since the differences are often very slight in their practical effect, it may be even more useful to consider the underlying similarity of these formulae. They all approach the condition of proportionate shares. Their divergence from that condition is considerable in each case, but the formulae are responsible only for marginal ranges of variation. The differences between P.R. formulae are blurred when district magnitude is allowed to vary. Indeed the mechanics of the formulae depend largely upon district magnitude. Any of these formulae will behave more like a different formula applied at the same level of district magnitude than like the same formula at a very different level of magnitude. For that reason I will consider P.R. formulae as a single class for many purposes. For some explanatory purposes, I will need to call upon the distinctions between these formulae, but this should not becloud the major perspective: P.R. formulae are generally similar to each other in practical effect.

The preceding pages have defined one of the three important properties shared by all electoral systems—the formulae of victory. Three main kinds of formulae have been discussed: majority, plurality, and proportional representation. The last class has, of course, proved the most heterogeneous and complex of the three. I have suggested that the three formulae differ in several respects, but that the most critical of these for party competition is probably relative proportionality. Plurality systems seem least likely to produce proportional results; majority systems appear to be intermediate; and P.R. formulae seem most likely to approximate proportionality.

At this point, it may be useful to move back from the detailed perspective into which the foregoing analysis has drawn us. Electoral formulae are only one of the three major aspects of any electoral law. Balloting types and district magnitudes are likely to have at least equal importance for interparty competition. In the next section, these variables are used to describe the electoral laws of twenty nations.

Electoral Laws

Variables and classifications are not themselves very informative; they are categories for describing the world, but alone they describe nothing. The variables already discussed remain empty of empirical content, and it is time to fill them with information about existing electoral systems.

As mentioned earlier, the study is based on the electoral practices of twenty nations during twenty years, 1945–

1965. I limited the range of the study to general parliamentary elections in these nations. In the pages which follow, the electoral laws governing these elections during this period in the specified countries are described in the categories elaborated earlier.

The data are summarized by Table 2.1 below. For each of the countries the state of each variable—balloting, districting, and electoral formula—is recorded. Where the state of a variable has changed during the postwar period, its condition is summarized chronologically within the appropriate cell. This 60-cell table is, of course, a complicated matrix. Its formal complexity is compounded by the enormous variation of the electoral laws it describes. Considering that the horizontal rows amount to capsule descriptions of electoral laws, it will be noticed that they fit into no general and homogeneous classes. With the exception of the four unadulterated Anglo-American laws found in Great Britain, the United States, Canada, and New Zealand, no two electoral laws are exactly alike.[34] This is the variation which necessitated a lengthy elaboration of variables, and it now forces us to examine the summary data in some detail.

It may be easier to see the major patterns of variation by sorting the laws into general classes. First, there are the four *Anglo-American* systems, with simple candidate ballots, single-member districts, and plurality formulae: Great Britain, the United States, New Zealand, and Canada. This class is by all odds the most homogeneous.

Second, there are seven electoral systems which may be classed together under the label *ordinary P.R.* These systems have simple party-list balloting, district magnitudes of about five, and proportional representation formulae, typically the d'Hondt highest averages variation. All indeed employ party-list ballots, but these allow various degrees of choice among the candidates on a single list, with Norway's

34. Iceland and Denmark also have very similar laws, because the Icelandic law is modeled after its Danish counterpart.

full intra-list preference the extreme case. Average district magnitudes vary from 2.2 in the earlier Icelandic system to 8.2 in the Swedish case. In three cases—Iceland, Austria, and Denmark—these districts are complex. In four other cases —Belgium, France (before 1958), Norway, and Sweden— the districts are simple. The proportional representation formulae are even less uniform, with both d'Hondt and Lague highest averages and largest remainder types represented. Despite these variations, the seven—Austria, Belgium, Denmark, France (before 1958), Iceland, Norway, and Sweden —form a class of systems all of which are modestly proportional.

Third, there are four systems—Finland, the Netherlands, Israel, and Italy—which may be called *large-district P.R.* These electoral laws also prescribe simple party-list ballots, except that Israel uses a party symbol ballot which has no listing of candidates. Each of the four uses a P.R. electoral formula, but no two are alike. The distinguishing feature of these systems is the fact that each has a very *high average district magnitude*. Finland's figure is lowest at 13.3; Italy's is 19.1; the Israeli and Dutch districting is national, so that the "averages" are 120 and 125[35] respectively. In each case, however, the magnitude is high enough to make the P.R. formula, whatever its type, operate to its fullest effect. These, in short, are laws likely to produce unusually close approximations of proportional results.[36]

Fourth, there are two systems, found in Switzerland and Luxembourg, which may be called *ordinal P.R.* systems. The distinguishing feature is, of course, the ordinal ballot: both Luxembourg and Switzerland use party-list ballots with cumulation and *panachage*. In effect, the voter is allowed to rank parties under these ballots. Average district

35. This figure reflects the 100-seat figure which prevailed before 1956 and the 150-seat total which prevailed thereafter in the Netherlands.

36. Because of its *imperiali* formula, Italy is likely to be the least proportional of the four cases.

TABLE 2.1
ELECTORAL LAWS, 1945 to 1965*

COUNTRY	BALLOT TYPE	DISTRICT MAGNITUDE**	FORMULA
Australia	ORDINAL: alternative candidate ballot	1.0	MAJORITY
Austria	CATEGORICAL: simple party-list ballot	5.7, complex	PROPORTIONAL REPRESENTATION: d'Hondt highest average
Belgium	CATEGORICAL: simple party-list ballot	7.1	PROPORTIONAL REPRESENTATION: d'Hondt highest average
Canada	CATEGORICAL: simple candidate ballot	1.0	PLURALITY
Denmark	CATEGORICAL: simple party-list ballot	6.7, complex	PROPORTIONAL REPRESENTATION: Lague highest average & largest remainder
Finland	CATEGORICAL: simple party-list ballot	13.3	PROPORTIONAL REPRESENTATION: d'Hondt highest average
France	CATEGORICAL 1945–57: simple parry-list ballot 1958–65: simple candidate ballot	1945–57: 6.7 approx. 1958–65: 1.0	1945–51: PROPORTIONAL REPRESENTATION: d'Hondt highest average 1951–57: PROPORTIONAL REPRESENTATION: d'Hondt highest average (Paris) and largest remainder (elsewhere). 1958–65: MAJORITY-PLURALITY: double ballot system.

West Germany	CATEGORICAL: simple candidate and party-list ballots	1949–53: 1.6, complex 1953–56: 1.9, complex 1956–65: 2.0, complex	PLURALITY and PROPORTIONAL REPRESENTATION: d'Hondt highest average
Great Britain	CATEGORICAL: simple candidate ballot	1.0	PLURALITY
Iceland	CATEGORICAL: simple party-list ballot	2.2, complex pre–1959 6.7, complex post–1959	PROPORTIONAL REPRESENTATION
Ireland	ORDINAL: alternative candidate ballot	3.7	PROPORTIONAL REPRESENTATION: Hare single transferable vote
Israel	CATEGORICAL: party ballot	120.0	PROPORTIONAL REPRESENTATION: before 1951: highest average after 1951: largest remainder
Italy	CATEGORICAL: simple party-list ballot	19.1	PROPORTIONAL REPRESENTATION: *Imperiali* largest remainder (65% bonus rule in 1953)
Luxembourg	ORDINAL: *panachage* with limited cumulation allowed	13.0	PROPORTIONAL REPRESENTATION: largest remainder

TABLE 2.1 (*Continued*)

COUNTRY	BALLOT TYPE	DISTRICT MAGNITUDE **	FORMULA
Netherlands	CATEGORICAL: simple party-list ballot	100.0 (pre–1956) 150.0 (post–1956)	PROPORTIONAL RERESENTATION
New Zealand	CATEGORICAL: simple candidate ballot	1.0	PLURALITY
Norway	CATEGORICAL: simple party-list ballot	7.5	PROPORTIONAL REPRESENTATION: d'Hondt highest average until 1953; Lague highest average after 1953
Sweden	CATEGORICAL: simple party-list ballot	8.2	PROPORTIONAL REPRESENTATION: Lague highest average
Switzerland	ORDINAL: *panachage* with cumulation allowed	8.0	PROPORTIONAL REPRESENTATION: d'Hondt highest average
U.S.A.	CATEGORICAL: simple candidate ballot	1.0	PLURALITY

* See Bibliography (Election Law Sources).
** Average values indicated.

magnitudes—13.0 for Luxembourg and 8.0 for Switzerland —are fairly high. Switzerland uses a d'Hondt formula, while Luxembourg uses a largest remainder. Luxembourg is therefore likely, with ordinal voting and largest remainder formula, to be the most hospitable of environments for small parties. Both systems allow the dispersion of votes among parties from the beginning—with the individual vote.

Four other systems fit nowhere in these classes, and each must be taken as a deviant case. The Irish single-transferable vote system, with the ordinal ballot, small districts (average magnitude 3.7), and the complicated Hare formula, was discussed earlier. The Fifth Republic French system is closer to the Anglo-American model than anything else, but cannot really be put there. The double-balloting, the complicated provision for alliances, and the rigid majority formula on the first ballot exclude it from the more prosaic Anglo-American class. The Australian law would also belong with its Anglo-American kin, except for the alternative candidate ballot and the majority formula. And the West German case is "half Anglo-American," since it provides for election of half the Bundestag by simple plurality in single-member districts with the simple candidate ballot. The use of P.R. formulae in a very large district—the *länder* before 1956, and all of West Germany since—forces me to classify it as a mixed system. These four cases are each classes unto themselves.

This classification is not at all satisfactory: its classes are neither exhaustive nor are the observations which they subsume homogeneous. This should not surprise us. Human institutions are the aggregate consequences of individual behavior, itself almost infinitely variable. And I am examining these products of behavior across national and cultural lines. Uniformity, not variation, should surprise us. Election laws simply do not conform to general, ideal-type classes.

For that reason, I will continue to treat the three variables —ballots, districts, and formulae—separately. This tactic allows me to be more precise without surrendering the cross-national scope of the study, since, for each of the three, a fairly clear typology has already been devised. The variables produce exhaustive treatment of the relevant electoral provisions within reasonably homogeneous classes. Accordingly, the substantive chapters of the study will take up these variables one at a time. At the end the analysis will be generalized a little further.

It should be pointed out that the foregoing discussion of electoral laws does not cover every provision of every law. Notably, it excludes provisions for interparty alliances and specific "cut-off" or penalty provisions aimed at very small or subversive parties. These provisions are common and are likely to be important in some situations. Yet they probably exert marginal pressures on party competition when considered along with the major variables considered here. Instead of further extending the present analysis to include all of these provisions, I have decided to treat them as a secondary set of variables. They will be invoked where a particular piece of analysis suggests their importance.

CHAPTER 3

POLITICAL PARTY SYSTEMS

The network of competitive relationships between political parties is what I mean by the term *political party system*. The party system is not literally a collection of parties—men, institutions, activities. It is instead the *competition* between these parties within a single political regime, and it is this system of competition (the party system) which gives to democratic political parties their unique importance. Political parties are the publicly identified minorities, the labeled groups, which compete for the right to govern.[1] And the party system is the matrix of competitive relationships between these parties. The party system is the whole assortment of interparty rivalries in a single country at any single time. And it is this web of competition which makes the whole number of parties in a country something more than they would be counted singly. That something more is democratic competition for the right to rule.

To talk accurately about party systems, it is essential to begin with some fairly precise measures which describe the competitive relationships between parties. These relationships call forth ideas like strength or weakness, equality or

1. Leon Epstein, "Political Parties in Western Democratic Systems," *Essays in Political Science*, ed. Edward H. Buehrig (Bloomington, Indiana University Press, 1966), p. 104.

inequality, success or failure, power or impotence. Operationally, these ideas converge upon two sets of data: party shares in the popular vote and party fractions (shares of seats) in parliaments. These are the legitimate artifacts of the right to rule and the actual authority to govern. Votes are claims upon seats under electoral laws, and seats are claims upon the authority to govern. It will therefore be fruitful to balance our ideas about party competition—hence, party systems—upon these data.

We are talking about two different party systems: (1) the *elective party system*, and (2) the *parliamentary* (*legislative*) *party system*. The former is a system of competitive relationships measured in votes, while the latter is a system of competitive relationships measured in parliamentary seats. The two are not unrelated, since the parliamentary system is formed from the elective system. If a child is modeled after the flesh of its parents under the rules of genetics, parliamentary party systems are developed from elective party systems according to the rules of the electoral system. The transformation is seldom, as I suggested earlier, a perfect one. Indeed many electoral laws produce recurring and systematic "mutations" or distortions in the translation of voting returns into allotments of parliamentary seats. But the *purpose* of election laws is the construction of the parliamentary party system out of the elective party system. Without forgetting their attachment to each other under the electoral law, I will examine these two subsystems of party competition individually, before returning in greater detail to the connection between them. The connection is, of course, very important to this study; it is the dynamic effect of electoral law.

Elective Party System Variables

In elections, political parties compete for votes. Their competitive positions are therefore measured in shares of the total vote (T):

$$T = \frac{\text{vote total for a given party}^2}{\text{vote total for all parties}}$$

In describing interparty competition, this quantity, the share of the vote won by any one party, will be centrally important. Any aggregate description of elective party systems will be constructed from concepts which are derived from it.[3] Party shares of the total vote are, in short, the basic data which describe the elective party system. Each of the five variables I have chosen to employ rests ultimately upon these vote shares. Together, they describe the overall texture of the competitive relationships between elective parties—the elective party system.

The Number of Parties (N_e)

How many parties received *any* votes? Is the total vote divided into few or many party shares? These questions call attention to the *number* of parties competing in an election, and this number becomes a variable in the present description of elective party systems (N_e). Its simplicity makes the number of parties an attractive variable. Its precise, quantitative nature also makes it useful for many analytic purposes. Yet the number of parties is not the most useful of the five variables used to describe elective party systems.

The number of parties may tell us how many competitive positions are to be considered but it tells nothing about the relative strengths of these positions. For example, the number of parties fails to distinguish between these three party systems:

	System One	*System Two*	*System Three*
Party A	90%	45%	34%
Party B	9%	40%	34%
Party C	1%	15%	32%
	100%	100%	100%

2. The capital letter T is used here since it refers to national, not district totals. Capital letter notation always refers to national data and small letters refer to district data.

3. For some purposes, these shares will be analyzed without further aggregation.

In each of the three cases, N equals three. Yet they represent very different sets of competitive relationships. In one, a single party enjoys obvious dominance; in another, two parties compete on rather even terms; in a third case, the three parties are all on about even terms. In short, the number of parties presents only the most rudimentary image of the elective party system.

The Vote Share of the Strongest Party (P_e)

What share of the vote is held by the strongest single party? In what degree does a single party dominate all of its competitors? These questions draw our attention to another variable: *the vote share of the strongest party* (P_e). If we adopt the convention of noting the parties from strongest to weakest in alphabetical order, this strongest party will always be "Party A." P_e may then be defined as the vote share of Party A, or:

$$P_e \equiv T_a$$

This variable provides new information which is not offered by the number of parties (N_e). Consider again the three party systems discussed above. N_e failed to distinguish between them, but P_e will show them as follows:

$$
\begin{array}{ll}
\text{System One:} & P_e = .90 \\
\text{System Two:} & P_e = .45 \\
\text{System Three:} & P_e = .34
\end{array}
$$

These figures suggest that the first example is a case of one-party dominance, which is indeed correct. It also suggests that the other two are systems without dominant parties, which is also true. There is little doubt that the variable is worthwhile, and it will indeed be relied upon in later analysis.

The share of the vote held by the strongest party is, however, a rather limited datum. It tells us nothing about the competitive positions of the second, third, fourth, or n^{th}

parties. For example, it gives us the same value for these two party systems:

	System One	System Two
Party A	45%	45%
Party B	44%	20%
Party C	11%	20%
Party D	—	15%
	100%	100%

In both cases, the strongest party has polled 45 per cent of the vote, so P_e equals .45.[4] But the two party systems are composed of very different competitive relationships. In "System One," two parties compete almost evenly; it is a "two-party system" very much like the actual British case. But "System Two" presents a different picture, with three almost equal opposition parties arrayed against a strong party which enjoys a dominant relationship to each of them, but not to the three combined. This variable (P_e) adds information to the raw number of parties, but is not itself a full description of the party system. It tells us nothing about the relative strengths of the lesser parties.

The Combined Vote Shares of the Two Strongest Parties (W_e)

What share of the vote is held by the *two* strongest parties? In what degree do the two strongest competitors dominate their weaker opponents? In what measure is it correct to describe a particular case as a "two-party system"? These questions suggest a third variable: *the combined vote shares of the two strongest parties* (W_e). This variable may be noted:

$$W_e = T_a + T_b$$

This variable draws upon a quantity ignored by P_e, namely the vote share of the second party. W_e therefore

4. N_e and other similar variables are presented here as decimal fractions, not per cents, because it is more useful in statistical analysis. For other purposes, it would be as useful to leave them in percentage form.

uses information previously wasted. Consider the first example for a third time (page 49 above). W_e produces values of .99, .85, and .68 for the three systems respectively (One, Two, Three). It tells us that lesser parties enjoy progressively weaker competitive positions in the three party systems. And, in a sense, this variable tells us how closely a system approaches the condition of two-party competition. It does not tell us how evenly the two compete with *each other*, but it does tell us the degree to which the two together dominate all comers. If we wish to describe the "two-party*ness*" of a system, this variable can be used effectively can be used effectively so long as it is safe to assume that *one* party does not hold a dominant share of the vote. This requires that the share of the first party (P_e) be controlled. A two-party system might, for some purposes, be defined by the conditions:

$$P_e < .70$$
$$W_e > .90$$

This rather simplistic definition of two-party competition will be of some use since it defines a population of systems in which two parties together poll most of the votes, and in which neither is altogether dominant over the other.

These three variables—the number of parties, the vote share of the strongest party, and the combined vote share of the two strongest parties—offer considerable descriptive power, but they focus our attention on only a few important dimensions of party competition. If party systems were icebergs, these variables would measure their total depth (the number of parties), and would tell us the proportion of this total which floats above the water's surface (the shares of the first two parties). But the general topography of the icebergs—the relative fragmentation of whole systems—would remain uncharted. It would be possible to remedy this shortcoming by adding more rather specific variables to measure all the facets of competition, but this proliferation of categories would soon complicate the description so greatly that general patterns would be hidden by specific ones. I would eventually be obliged to synthesize general categories from specific ones in order to examine these more general, and therefore more interesting, relationships. For that reason, it seems sensible to introduce a variable which describes the general structure of competitive relationships at this point. This variable, which may be called "fractionalization" (as opposed to concentration), is meant to provide wide-angle snapshots of party systems.

The Fractionalization of Vote Shares (F_e)

Is competitive strength concentrated in one party, or is it divided among many parties? Is this a "one-party system," a "two-party system," a "three-party system," or an extreme variety of "multi-partism"? In short, how extensively is competitive strength dispersed among contestants? These important questions call for general descriptions of competitive relationships resting upon the positions of *all* the parties. They call for a measure of *fractionalization*.

The idea of fractionalization resolves itself into two lesser concepts: (1) the number of party shares,[5] and (2) the relative equality of these shares. A non-fractionalized system has only one share, and that share contains the whole pool of competitive power; this is the "one-party system," which entails no competitive relationships. Its concrete analog is a whole apple. *A highly fractionalized system has a great many shares of about equal magnitude so that no one of them contains a very large share of the total pool of strength* (i.e. votes). This corresponds to an extreme case of "multi-partism," with, say, ten parties, each polling about one tenth of the total vote. Its concrete analog is an apple which has been sliced into ten equal pieces, no one of which is anything like the size of the original apple. Fractionalization varies by degrees, between the whole apple and the

5. This quantity is (N_e).

ready ingredients of an apple pie. Fractionalization means division into many parts, and all the actual party systems are fractionalized to *some* degree.[6]

Fractionalization cannot be equated with the number of parties (N_e). The relative equality of party shares, whatever their number, is also an integral part of the concept. Consider two systems with three parties each:

	System One	*System Two*
A:	90%	34%
B:	6%	33%
C:	4%	33%

Both systems contain three parties or, more exactly, three shares of the total vote. But System Two is much more fractionalized: the three shares are about equal so that no one of them approaches the total vote. System One is much less fractionalized, since the shares are very unequal, so that one of them comes within 10 per cent of the total vote. System One is like an apple which remains whole, except for two slivers which have been shaved away. System Two, on the other hand, resembles an apple which has been sliced into three chunks, none of which has nearly the bulk of the original fruit. The number of shares (or parties) does not *determine* the extent of fractionalization. This number is instead the *limiting* factor upon fractionalization: a given number of shares can attain only a certain degree of fractionalization. That maximum is reached when the shares are perfectly equal, and the maximum limit increases with the number of shares.

Despite its superficial duplicity, this variable forms a continuum; any party system falls at some single point along the continuum between the extremes of concentration (non-fractionalization) and infinite fractionalization.[7] This

6. I am putting aside intraparty factionalism here.

7. Two non-identical systems may, both conceptually and operationally, have the same level of fractionalization. One might have more par-

is the continuum which lies unstated between one-party
and extreme multi-party competition:

	one-	two-	three-	extreme
Party-System:	party	party	party	multi-party
Fractionalization:	none	intermediate		extreme

This parallel is clearer if we recognize that the conventional
terms—"one-party," "two-party," "multi-party"—are
never understood literally.[8] System One (above, page 54)
would be called "one-party," despite its having three parties,
because the bulk of the vote is concentrated in one party's
share. The actual British system is called a "near two-party
system" because only two parties have substantial shares,
yet as many as a dozen parties often get *some* share of the
vote. This conventional language is an inexact device for
expressing degrees of fractionalization. It does not cope well
with intermediate cases and small differences. It is a primi-
tive shorthand used to suggest the infinite variation of competitive relationships in actual party systems.

If I quantify the fractionalization continuum, it will sensitize this analysis to the many subtle variations found in
actual elective party systems. The means by which this
quantification is accomplished are described below.

The model of party system fractionalization proposed
here is based on the probability that any two randomly selected voters will have chosen different parties in any given
election. It is, in effect, an indicator of the frequency with
which pairs of voters would disagree if an entire electorate

---

ties competing on rather unequal terms, while another equally fractionalized system might have fewer parties competing on more nearly equal
terms.

8. It must be understood that I am presently abstracting one element—
competition—from a complex whole. The degree to which the leaders
of the parties are willing to bargain with each other (as opposed to hos-
tile intransigence) would be an important consideration which is ignored
for analytic purposes here.

interacted randomly. In addition to the theoretical interest
of this frequency, the model offers a number of advantages
for the present analysis. First, it is sensitive to both the number and the relative equality of the party shares. Second, it
will allow us to consider systems with any number of parties, and to compare the resulting states of fractionalization
with those which are obtained for legislative party systems.
And third, it may prove to be a convenient device for other
students who wish to examine the general concept of fractionalization in other contexts.

The model is derived from simple probability statistics.
The chance that our two voters will have chosen the *same*
party is approximated by the sum of the squared decimal
shares of the vote obtained by all parties:

$$\text{Probability of Dyadic Agreement} = \sum_{i=1}^{n} T_i^2$$

(Where T_i = any party's decimal share of the vote)

It follows that the probability of dyadic disagreement (here
labelled F_e) is the complement of this quantity:

$$F_e = 1 - \left(\sum_{i=1}^{n} T_i^2 \right)$$

The resulting values are used here to indicate the extent
of party system fractionalization. An examination of Table
3.1, in which sample values are computed for several hypothetical party systems, will demonstrate that this index produces values which are consistent with the concept of fractionalization. Superficially, this is because the formula is
sensitive to the components of the concept—the number
and relative equality of vote shares. More fundamentally, the
formula and the concept are congruent because both are
aspects of the same phenomenon: interparty disagreement.
The party shares of the vote are indicators of this competi-

TABLE 3.1
SAMPLE VALUES FOR FRACTIONALIZATION
Party Shares

System	F_e Value	T_a	T_b	T_c	T_d	T_e	T_f	T_g	$T_h \ldots T_n$
A	0.0	1.0	—	—					
B	0.18	0.9	0.1						
C	0.32	0.8	0.2						
D	0.48	0.6	0.4						
E	0.50	0.5	0.5						
F	0.58	0.5	0.4	0.1					
G	0.62	0.5	0.3	0.2					
H	0.64	0.4	0.4	0.2					
I	0.67	0.33	0.33	0.33					
J	0.70	0.4	0.3	0.2	0.1				
K	0.75	0.25	0.25	0.25	0.25				
L	0.80	0.2	0.2	0.2	0.2	0.2			
M	0.875	0.125	0.125	0.125	0.125	0.125	0.125	0.125	0.125

tive nexus; the fractionalization index is a simple abstraction from the same nexus, which is related to the party shares by simple algebra.

The fractionalization values occupy a continuum, running from non-fractionalization in perfect one-party systems (F_e equals zero) to *complete* fractionalization—an event never occurring in reality or the formula—defined by the limiting F_e value of unity. Under a perfect one-party regime, there is no fractionalization, and no two voters could have chosen different parties (hence, F_e equals zero). Under a perfect two-party (i.e. 50-50 split) system, an intermediate form of fractionalization exists, and there is an even chance that two voters will have chosen different parties (hence, F_e equals 0.5). In an imaginary system where each voter chooses his own "party," an extreme form of fractionalization exists, and any pair of voters would necessarily have disagreed (hence, F_e approaches unity). The reader will see that the intermediate spaces are filled by values on the same continuum (Table 3.1).

The properties of this index may be summarized as follows:

1. The values range between the limits of zero and one.
2. The values may be treated as components of an interval scale, with a fixed zero point (sometimes called a ratio scale).
3. The values are consistent with the concept of fractionalization.
4. The measure may be applied to any party system, whatever the total number of parties.
5. The measure is sensitive to all the data: each party's share is included (although in practice those with shares below .005 are eliminated).
6. The same measure may be used for legislative party systems, by substituting seat shares for vote shares. And it could, in principle, be applied to other sorts of cleavages (i.e., linguistic, religious, racial, etc.).

Since I am discussing elective party systems at present, it will be useful to distinguish *elective* fractionalization by the subscript "e." Elective fractionalization is thus noted F_e. Its parliamentary counterpart (F_p) will occupy our attention later on.

This variable (F) should provide a very flexible measure of fractionalization in party systems. It should, in short, produce fairly crisp "snapshots" with a wide field of vision. But they will necessarily be just that—snapshots taken in static time perspective. With this, and the three variables mentioned earlier, it will be possible to describe conditions accurately at any one time, but they will not sensitize our thinking to relative degrees of stability. For that a fifth and final variable is required.

Average Change of Vote Shares (E_e)

Does the competitive outcome of this election reflect a radical alteration of earlier election outcomes, or have party positions remained pretty much unchanged? Have the fortunes of the parties reversed themselves, or have they remained stable? [9] These questions require a measure of rela-

9. Since parties are identified only by rank in the previous variables, they are not sensitive to changes in the performances of actual parties. They relate competitive positions, not particular parties. This variable is a remedy.

tive stability, which is here operationalized inversely as the "average change" of the party vote shares (E_e).

This variable rests upon a comparison of the distribution of party shares in an election with the same distribution as the last previous election. Unlike the other four variables, this one rests on the vote shares of parties identified *by name*, not by rank. To compare changes in rank positions, the other variables can simply be extended; to compare the stability of actual party performances, this new measure is needed. The operational question therefore becomes, "How much have the vote shares of the parties changed since the last election?" The absolute differences in shares of the vote for all of the parties are thus computed and totaled. This sum, representing the absolute total change of party shares, is then divided by the number of parties to produce the average change *per* party.[10]

Consider two examples, the first for a very stable situation and the second for an unstable one:

System One:

Parties	% Vote T_1	% Vote T_2	% Change	Average % Change
Red	40	39	1	
Blue	39	40	1	
Green	21	21	0	
	100	100	Sum = 2	$\frac{2}{3} = 0.67\%$

System Two:

Parties	% Vote T_1	% Vote T_2	% Change	Average % Change
White	50	20	30	
Yellow	30	40	10	
Pink	20	40	20	
	100	100	Sum = 60	$\frac{60}{3} = 20\%$

The vote shares of the parties, and therefore their relative competitive positions, have changed little in System One.

---

10. The measure focuses on the later of two elections, so the number of parties (if it has changed) is taken from the later case. Parties with fewer than 2% of the vote in the focal election are excluded.

Its average change figure (0.67%) is therefore low. But the shares have been jumbled in System Two, which is a case of unstable competition. The average change figure here is accordingly a high one (20%). These figures record relative stability of average party shares.

These then are the five variables used to measure the shapes of elective party systems. Before turning to the application of these variables, another parallel set of categories is needed: parliamentary party system variables.

Parliamentary Party Systems

The basic component of party competition in legislatures or parliaments is the parliamentary seat. A party's relative strength is a function of its share of the total seats, better known as its "delegation," or "fraction." These parcels of competitive advantage are computed:

$$S = \frac{\text{number of seats held by a party}}{\text{total seats in parliament}}$$

This quantity (S) is exactly analogous to the quantity used for the comparison of elective parties (T): seats have simply been substituted for votes. It is therefore apparent that the two units of analysis—seat shares (S) and vote shares (T)—may be manipulated similarly. For that reason, all five of the elective system variables may be transposed into the parliamentary context, which is doubly useful: (1) it offers a conceptual economy, and (2) it permits exact comparisons of the two competitive systems, elective and parliamentary.[11] While it will be necessary to add a sixth variable to measure minimal majorities in parliamentary systems, these five transposed variables will require only very brief examination since their mechanics have already been described above.

11. Parliamentary variables are identified by the subscript "p," as opposed to "e," which identifies elective variables.

The Number of Parliamentary Parties (N_p)

How many parties have actually won a seat in parliament? This question asks simply for the number of parliamentary parties (N_p), a quantity exactly parallel to the number of elective parties (N_e). A comparison of the two variables will offer evidence about the degree to which the electoral system has penalized certain parties, usually the very small ones.

The Seat Share of the Strongest Party (P_p)

What proportion of the parliament's seats are concentrated in the hands of the single strongest party? That is, what is the seat share of the strongest parliamentary party (P_p)? This variable is exactly parallel to the vote share of the strongest elective party (P_e), and is computed by identity from S_a (the seat share of the strongest party):

$$P_p \equiv S_a$$

A comparison of P_p and P_e should indicate the relative advantage given to the strongest party by an electoral law.

The Combined Seat Shares of the Two Strongest Parties (W_p)

What proportion of the parliament's seats are concentrated in the hands of the *two* strongest parties? How closely does the parliamentary party system approach the minimal condition of two-party competition? These questions are answered for any parliamentary party system by the variable (W_p) which is the combined shares of seats held by the first two parties:

$$W_p = S_a + S_b$$

This variable is, of course, analogous to (W_e) which is applied to elective party systems. A comparison of the two will tell the analyst what is happening under a given electoral system to these stronger parties.

The Fractionalization of Seat Shares (F_p)

Is parliamentary authority (i.e. seats) concentrated in one party or is it divided among many parties? Is this a one-party, two-party, or multi-party parliamentary system? These questions ask for a measure of fractionalization in parliamentary systems (F_p). The measure is exactly parallel—conceptually and computationally—to the fractionalization of elective party systems. It is computed from the seat shares as follows:

$$F_p = 1 - \left(\sum_{i=2}^{n} Si^2 \right)$$

A comparison of fractionalization in parliamentary and elective systems will indicate the extent to which an electoral system defractionalizes or condenses the distribution of strength in converting votes to seats. This seems likely to be a very important phenomenon, which may be measured exactly by this pairing of variables.[12]

Average Change of Seat Shares (E_p)

Does this distribution of parliamentary seats reflect a radical alteration of the distribution which existed after the last previous election? Have the relative fortunes of the parties changed? These questions require a measure of relative stability, offered here as the average change of seat shares (E_p) —which is an inverse index of stability. It is exactly analogous to (E_e), and is computed in the same manner by substituting seat shares (S) for vote shares (T). A comparison of the two may help to measure the degrees to which electoral laws exaggerate or damp the effects of changes in elective competition.

Minimal Parliamentary Majority (A)

How many parties are required for the formation of a majority coalition in parliament? Assuming full freedom of

12. Since our measure indicates the probability of paired disagreements with respect to party, this may be especially useful for legislative analysis.

combination (alliance), how many partners are needed in the bargain of governing? What, in short, is the minimal majority, measured in the number of parties composing it (A)? This variable has no analog in the elective system; its special importance follows from the special importance of majorities *inside* parliament. It is computed simply by counting the number of party shares required to reach a combined share of more than 0.5. Consider three examples:

Parliament One	Parliament Two	Parliament Three	
A: 55%	A: 45%	A: 20%	
B: 40%	B: 40%	B: 19%	
C: 5%	C: 15%	C: 15%	
		D: 15%	
		E: 14%	
		F: 10%	
		G: 7%	

In the first case the minimal majority is one; in the second it is two; and in the third it is three.[13] These differences are likely to be very important in the behavior of parliamentary party leaders who seek to build majorities in order to govern. They are also, and for the same reasons, likely to relate closely to the relative stability of cabinets in various systems.

* * *

Party systems—networks of competitive relationships between political parties—have two important aspects: (1) elective, and (2) parliamentary or legislative. In elective party systems, the vote is the essential unit of competitive advantage; in parliamentary party systems, the seat is the essential unit. Between these two aspects of party competition lies the functional domain of electoral laws: the conversion of elective outcomes into parliamentary party systems. By the direction and degree to which an electoral law modifies elective outcomes in the process of translating votes to seats, the electoral law will influence the structure of the party system in parliament. This will be called the

13. Three is the largest observed value. Two is the most common.

"proximal impact" of electoral laws on party systems; by systematic repetition of similar modifications over time, an electoral law may influence both parliamentary *and* elective systems at future dates. This effect will be called "the distal impact" of electoral laws, and it will be investigated later.

This chapter has been used to define eleven variables which make these inferences possible. Ten of these variables belong to five pairs with a member applied to elective competition and a member applied to parliamentary competition. Another, the minimal majority variable, is applied only to parliamentary systems. The variables are:

1 and 2: the number of parties (N), both elective (N_e) and parliamentary (N_p)

3 and 4: the competitive share of the strongest party (P), in votes (P_e) and in seats (P_p)

5 and 6: the combined competitive shares of the two strongest parties (W), in votes (W_e) or in seats (W_p)

7 and 8: the fractionalization of party systems (F), both elective (F_e) and parliamentary (F_p)

9 and 10: the average change of party shares in competitive advantage between two elections (E), in the elective sphere (E_e) or in the parliamentary sphere (E_p)

11: the minimal majority, or the smallest number of parties required to form a majority coalition in parliament (M_p)

These variables describe party systems, just as the variables explained in Chapter 2 describe electoral laws. At issue is the empirical relationship between the two: what effects do electoral laws have on party competition? To answer the question, attention must now turn toward the data themselves.

PART II

ANALYSIS

INTRODUCTION

By elaborating and defining the variables, Part I set the stage for the analysis presented here. In this section, four questions are analyzed by relating those variables to actual electoral laws and party systems: (1) In what ways do electoral systems exert similar effects upon party competition? (2) What differences mark the effects of various *electoral formulae?* (3) What seem to be the effects of variations in *district magnitudes?* (4) What differences in party competition seem to result from ordinal as opposed to categorical *balloting?*

These analyses will require two main kinds of inference from the data. The first pertains to the *proximal* effects of electoral laws upon party competition. These effects are inferred by comparing vote distributions in elections with the seat distributions following upon the same elections. If the proportions of the parties are identical in elective and legislative arenas, the electoral law has operated with complete proportionality, leaving competitive relationships between parties unaltered. It would therefore have exerted *no* proximal effect of its own upon party competition. If, however, as is always the case, the electoral system alters these party shares of seats as opposed to vote shares, then it will have exerted a proximal effect upon party competition. These proximal effects may be inferred with great confidence, since no intervening factors, save corruption, can possibly influence seat distributions after the votes are tabulated and submitted to the arbitration of the electoral law.[1]

The second sort of inference pertains to the *distal* (or long-range) effects of electoral laws upon party competition. These effects are inferred by comparing the elective or parliamentary party systems associated with various electoral laws. If, for example, single-member plurality electoral laws were always associated with two-party competition, then it might be inferred that this electoral system causes two-party competition. Inferences of this kind must be made with the *greatest* caution, since observed associations may reflect the influence of intervening or underlying factors in the political system which are independent of electoral law. Only probabilistic generalizations can therefore be made, even after careful analysis of fairly complete data.

The five chapters which follow build upon inferences of these two types to answer the four questions stated at the beginning of this introduction. The first deals with the shared effects of all electoral systems.

1. Corruption is ignored in my analysis on the ground that it is probably very rare in general elections. Needless to say, no data are available on corruption.

CHAPTER 4

GENERALLY SHARED EFFECTS

The influence of electoral systems could be compared to a brake or an accelerator. The multiplication of parties which arises from other factors is facilitated by one type of electoral system and hindered by another.

Maurice Duverger[1]

Most electoral systems work to the advantage of parties which obtain large shares of the popular vote and to the disadvantage of parties which obtain only modest shares of the vote. They tend, therefore, to act as "brakes" upon the fractionalization of party systems by favoring a few strong parties at the expense of many weaker ones. Some electoral systems are less violently prejudiced in favor of large parties than others, but all of them seem at least slightly biased in that direction. It follows that no electoral systems positively accelerate the development of small parties, but some are weaker brakes against their development than others. The propositions examined in this chapter explain and verify these speculative ideas.

1. *Political Parties* (New York, John Wiley and Sons, 1963), p. 205.

Six Similarity Propositions

> SIMILARITY PROPOSITION ONE: *Electoral systems tend to award more than proportionate shares of parliamentary seats to parties with large shares of the vote, and to award less than proportionate shares of seats to parties with smaller shares of the vote.*[2]

If this proposition is correct, strong elective parties will receive even more than the large shares of seats to which they are proportionally entitled, and weak elective parties will receive even less than the already small proportions of seats which they appear to have earned. These two tendencies may be stated:

1. for large parties: vote share (T) < seat share (S)
2. for small parties: vote share (T) > seat share (S)

The data strongly suggest that these conditions are usually fulfilled and that Proposition One is correct. Consider Figure 4.1, a scattergram which shows the relationship of seat shares to vote shares for 664 parties, each with at least 2 per cent of the vote, in 115 elections. If electoral systems showed no systematic bias, the broken line representing the exact equality of vote and seat shares would express the relationship of the two variables. As the data clearly demonstrate, that is not the case. The actual regression line, computed from a least-squares equation, suggests a systematic bias in favor of parties with large vote shares and against parties with small vote shares. The exact regression may be noted:

$$S = 1.13\,T - .0238$$

The bias is a gentle one: as vote shares (T) are increased, seat shares (S) increase at a slightly greater rate.[3] A unit of

2. For reasons revealed later on, "large" is apt to mean more than 20%, and "small" means less than 20%.

3. As Chapter 5 will show, proportional representation does not undo, but lessens, this general bias.

increase in vote shares corresponds to 1.13 units of increase in seat shares, after a constant of .0238 units has been de-

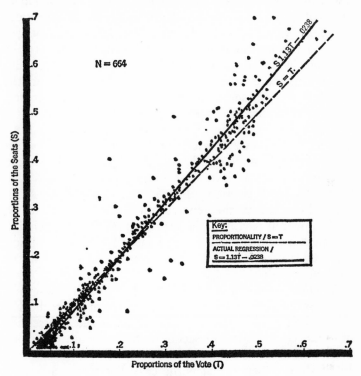

Figure 4.1

PROPORTIONS OF THE SEATS (s) PLOTTED AGAINST
PROPORTIONS OF THE VOTE (T): 664 PARTY
TRANSACTIONS IN 115 ELECTIONS *

ducted. For small parties, the constant is especially important, since the constant penalty is not fully counteracted

* The elections analyzed here are listed, by nation and date, in Appendix C. Those included are the 115 for which all data were available. Deviant dots are enlarged for emphasis.

until the vote share reaches 0.1993, or about 20 per cent of the vote. The vote share 0.2 is thus the breaking point, below which parties tend to receive less than proportionate shares of seats, and above which they generally receive more than proportionate shares of seats. Hence, the disadvantaged small parties are usually those with less than 20 per cent of the vote, and the advantaged large parties are typically those with more than 20 per cent of the vote. And the farther party vote shares diverge from this point, the greater tends to be the penalty imposed or the bonus granted.

A closer examination of the scattergram will reveal numerous exceptions to these generalizations. It must be accordingly understood clearly that the regression I have been examining is not a "law," but a generalization about what happens in *most* elections. That is why Proposition One is worded cautiously: the generalization is about a tendency, not a universal law. And the data confirm that the generalization expresses a fairly general fact of electoral politics: electoral laws tend to add to the advantage of strong parties over weak ones.

It should be noted in passing that some of the most conspicuous exceptions are as much apparent as real. The cluster below the regression line at about the intersection of $T = .45$ and $S = .40$ seems to be made up of strong parties receiving less than proportionate shares of the seats. In an absolute sense, that is the case. But these parties are mostly those which finished second to even stronger parties in two-party systems. For that reason, their loss is not the gain of very small parties but of even larger ones. Even if this cluster of apparently exceptional cases is discounted, it must be concluded that Proposition One states something less than an invariate relationship. A more specific proposition admits fewer exceptions:

SIMILARITY PROPOSITION TWO: *Electoral systems almost always award more than a proportionate share of the seats to the party which polls the largest single share of the vote.*

In other words, the first party's seat share (P_p) almost always exceeds its vote share (P_e):

$$P_p > P_e$$

In 106 of the 117 cases analyzed, this proposition proved correct. It is, in other words, correct in 90.5 per cent of the elections analyzed. As the proposition itself suggests, electoral systems *almost always* give a bonus to the strongest single party. But how large is the bonus? The question is answered in part by two data:

$$P_p = 0.468$$
$$P_e = 0.430$$
average difference $= \overline{0.038} = 3.8\%$ of the seats

The average bonus given the strongest party is 3.8 per cent of the total seats. It is safe to conclude that Proposition Two is substantially correct.

The eleven exceptional cases are concentrated in only four countries: Iceland (5), Denmark (3), Finland (2), and France (1). The ten Scandinavian cases occurred under proportional representation formulae, and the penalties imposed upon the first parties were slight. The French case was produced by a blatant and very effective effort to reduce the Communist delegation to the National Assembly in 1951; the party received 26.5 per cent of the vote, but only 19.6 per cent of the seats. In none of these cases was a party denied a legislative majority after it had won a majority of the votes, and in most cases the party was at least 20 percentage points short of a majority in votes.

If it is agreed that the strongest party is at least modestly advantaged by almost all electoral systems, it is still legitimate to question this fact's political significance. Proposition

Three deals with an extremely important consequence of the first party's bonus:

> SIMILARITY PROPOSITION THREE: *Most single-party parliamentary majorities are "manufactured" by electoral systems.*

Since most legislative decisions—including the decision to sustain a parliamentary government—are taken under the majority formula, the achievement of majority control in legislatures is very important. These parliamentary majorities may be achieved by a party in two ways: (1) by winning a majority of the popular vote and receiving a proportionate share of the seats, or (2) by winning less than a majority of the vote, but receiving a bonus of seats great enough to produce a majority. The first type may be considered an *earned* majority; the second type is a *manufactured* majority, in which the majority party has received a critical majority-forming bonus under the electoral system. Likewise, it is possible for a party to fail to obtain a legislative majority in two ways: (1) by winning too few votes and obtaining only a proportionate share of the vote, and (2) by winning a majority of the vote, but being penalized so severely by the electoral system that a majority of seats is not forthcoming. The first type is a *natural* minority, and the second is an *artificial* minority. These four outcomes are related to each other by Table 4.1:

TABLE 4.1
TYPES OF MAJORITY/MINORITY REPRESENTATION

		SEATS	$N = 117$
		$P_p > .5$	$P_p < .5$
VOTES	$P_e > .5$	*earned majorities* 16	*artificial minorities* 0
	$P_e < .5$	27 *manufactured* *majorities*	74 *natural minorities*

These data demonstrate a number of interesting patterns. First, no artificial minorities exist: it would be intolerable if an electoral law robbed leading parties of their majorities, and no such electoral systems exist.[4] Second, earned majorities are quite uncommon: only sixteen are found, and these are concentrated in four countries: the United States (8), Australia (4), New Zealand (3), and Canada (1). Third, natural minorities are very common: 74 of the 117 parliaments analyzed did without one-party majorities.

Last, and most important, manufactured majorities are quite common: they account for 27 of the 43 majorities, or 62.5 per cent of the one-party parliamentary majorities observed. Most parliamentary majorities are indeed manufactured by the bonus seats given to leading parties under electoral laws. These majority parties enjoy a position of legislative authority which is qualitatively greater than their vote totals would suggest, since the majority is itself so important. The majority, after all, entitles a party to all of the legislative authority, at least in parliamentary regimes. Their majorities confound any simple interpretation of the majority rule prescription so often taken for granted by democratic theory and by practical discourse. They suggest a positive consequence of electoral law seldom analyzed: *electoral laws may create majorities where none are created by the voters.*

This phenomenon is not associated only with plurality systems. It is true that 17 of the 27 manufactured majorities were produced by single-member plurality systems, but it is also true that the remaining ten were produced by seven different systems of proportional representation. The plurality systems which manufactured majorities were Great Britain (6), New Zealand (4), Canada (3), Australia (2), and the United States (2). The proportional representation

4. It is theoretically *possible* to produce this result under any electoral system with very low district magnitudes. As the data show, this possibility is never actualized.

systems producing similar majorities were Norway (4), Austria (1), Belgium (1), West Germany (1), Ireland (1), Italy (1), and Luxembourg (1). In all, twelve nations have relied upon these majorities, some of them—Britain, New Zealand, Norway—rather consistently.

The manufactured majority seems to be very general in its occurrence. Indeed, no leading party which received 48 per cent of the vote or more in any election failed to attain a legislative majority. Some parties, like the Norwegian Labor Party in the election of 1945, received majorities of seats with vote shares as low as 40 per cent. And the bonuses supplied to these parties were often large: in 1949, the Canadian Liberals received over 73 per cent of the seats in return for less than 50 per cent of the vote. It seems that elections are like horseshoe games: coming close is often as good as hitting the target directly, and near elective majorities often supply actual legislative ones.

The British case is especially interesting. The mother of parliaments, in which cohesive majorities have been an institutional necessity for many decades, apparently relies entirely upon manufactured majorities. Neither the Tories nor the Laborites can hope to win popular majorities because a considerable part of the vote is always drained off by minor parties, especially by the Liberals. Yet the electoral system always—in each of the six elections examined —provides a bonus for the leading party large enough to give it a majority in the House of Commons. These manufactured majorities appear to provide the functional equivalent of unadulterated two-party competition, and it seems likely that the British system would be a very different one in the absence of these manufactured majorities. The position of the Liberals and the other minority parties would certainly be stronger, since coalition governments would be required.[5]

5. This may explain the very considerable sympathy of the Liberal party for the P.R. reform movement in Great Britain.

It is fair to conclude that Proposition Three is sustained by the data: most parliamentary majorities are manufactured by electoral laws. These manufactured majorities seem to emerge from a wide variety of electoral systems and competitive situations. And they may be important to the legislative politics of the countries in which they occur: Britain was examined separately, but Norway, New Zealand, and Canada could have been singled out as well.

If these leading parties are awarded disproportionately large shares of parliamentary seats, other less successful parties must in turn receive disproportionately small parcels of seats. Parties which finish second or worse are necessarily penalized by the bonus of the leading party; if the leading party gets more than its apparent due, the lesser parties must receive even less than their apparent due. This suggests that some parties are left without *any* representation in legislatures:

> SIMILARITY PROPOSITION FOUR: *Electoral laws often limit the number of legislative parties by granting* no *seats to small parties, especially those which finish last in the popular voting.*

The data allow only a partial verification of this proposition, because the vote totals of very small parties are quite often omitted from tabulations in the press, and are sometimes officially reported in anonymous groups labeled "others." It is therefore likely that my data underestimate the number of small parties contesting some elections, and many parties are therefore denied representation without my knowing it. If anything, this source of error will make the proposition appear less persuasive than is in fact the case. Operationally, I am dealing with losing parties which managed to obtain vote shares no lower than one half of one per cent. For that reason, the following analysis concerns the elimination of *non-trivial* parties, and ignores tiny splinter groups as well as individual, independent candidacies.

How frequently is the weakest party denied representation? In 115 elections, this event occurred 74 times: 64.3 per cent of the last place parties were therefore denied representation. In Proposition Four, then, "often" may be interpreted as "nearly two thirds of the time," and the proposition appears to be substantially correct.

The weakest parties were not alone in their plight. In 30 of the same 115 elections the data show that at least two weak parties were similarly eliminated. In 21 elections three or more parties were dismissed, and 13 elections did away with four or more potential parliamentary parties. Other weak parties are often denied representation along with the *weakest* parties.

Is the elimination of weak parties a *unique* function of plurality electoral systems? The answer is no: 32 of the 74 elections in which the weakest party was denied representation took place under some variety of proportional representation.[6] These 32 cases were dispersed through the elections of twelve nations using P.R.—Austria, Belgium, Denmark, Finland, France, West Germany, Iceland, Israel, Italy, Luxembourg, the Netherlands, and Norway.

If it is admittedly true that P.R. systems usually place the "threshold of representation" lower than most plurality systems, why were many small parties eliminated under P.R.? The answer probably hinges upon something which could be called "anticipated failure." Under plurality systems, the leaders of actual or potential small parties may conclude that they cannot possibly win any seats, and decide not to nominate candidates. Under P.R. laws, comparable leaders may decide, incorrectly in many cases, that the threshold is low enough to give them at least a few seats. Hence, P.R. systems are faced with a larger number of small parties in elections, and even their relatively low

6. Nevertheless, as is shown by Differential Proposition Five, below, the elimination of weak parties is much more common under plurality formulae than under P.R. formulae.

thresholds are high enough to eliminate a number of them.

This brings me to a further conjecture: the perceived effects of electoral systems may be just as important as their actual consequences. Electoral systems thought to do violence to small parties will eliminate them *before* the election because their leaders decide against the contest. The idea that an electoral system refuses representation to small parties becomes a self-fulfilling hypothesis, because it causes leaders of small parties—or persons tempted to form them—to conclude that they cannot hope to obtain representation. This speculation is not verifiable, at least on the basis of available data. However that may be, Proposition Four seems to be substantially correct, for both plurality and P.R. electoral systems. The weakest parties are very often denied representation.

All of the foregoing propositions suggest a more general pattern. Electoral systems generally tend to: (1) advantage strong parties, especially those holding majorities or near-majorities, (2) disadvantage the weakest parties, and (3) withhold seats from weak parties, thereby reducing the total number of legislative parties. Can these findings be generalized through an analysis of party system fractionalization? The answer appears to be yes:

SIMILARITY PROPOSITION FIVE: *Electoral systems de-fractionalize parliamentary party systems.*

Operationally, this proposition means that parliamentary party systems will always be less fractionalized than the corresponding elective party systems. The legislative parties will be fewer and on the whole stronger than the elective parties. The seats will therefore be less fractionalized than the votes in each election:

$$F_p < F_e$$

This condition obtains in 112 of the 115 elections for which data are available. In only three cases is the parlia-

mentary party system more fractionalized than the elective
party system. Two of these exceptional elections, one Israeli
and one Icelandic, are very minor exceptions, both deviating
by less than .006 units of fractionalizations. The third was
produced in the French election of 1951, and its substantial
deviation (.209 units) results from the success with which a
number of small and middle-sized parties penalized the large
Communist party. With these three exceptions, Proposition
Five appears universal.

A more precise understanding of this defractionalization
process may be obtained by examining Figure 4.2 below. If
electoral systems tended to fractionalize parliamentary
party systems, most of the cases would appear above the
broken line at the center of the chart. Only the three exceptional cases I have mentioned are plotted above that line.
If, on the other hand, electoral systems had no systematic
effect upon fractionalization, the dots would cluster about
that same broken line, which is not the case. The dots are
in fact clustered along the actual regression plotted *below*
the broken line, meaning that electoral laws tend toward the
predicted *de*fractionalizing effect. The regression for this
pattern is:

$$F_p = 0.95 \, F_e - 0.0004 \text{ (Nil)}$$

Whether the elective competition is highly fractionalized
or not, the electoral laws will render the parliamentary
party systems less fractionalized than their elective counterparts. As elective fractionalization increases, parliamentary fractionalization increases at a lower rate. A unit increase for F_e produces 0.95 units increase in F_p. Hence, the
amount of *de*fractionalization increases gently as elective
fractionalization increases. And, at all levels of fractionalization for which actual cases exist, this defractionalization
tends to be substantial.

Different electoral systems, of course, produce different
degrees of defractionalization. But all of these differences

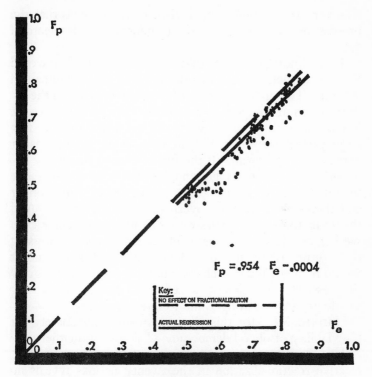

Figure 4.2
ELECTIVE FRACTIONALIZATION (F_e) PLOTTED
AGAINST PARLIAMENTARY OR LEGISLATIVE
FRACTIONALIZATION (F_p): 115 ELECTIONS *

* See Appendix C for a list of the elections included. They are the 115 with complete data.

involve degree, not direction, since none will fractionalize parliamentary party systems by comparison to their elective counterparts.

The data are unequivocal about Proposition Five: electoral systems defractionalize parliamentary or legislative party systems by comparison to their elective counterparts.

The very small number of deviant cases confirms that the process of defractionalization is general to all electoral systems.

These findings suggest that *elective* competition would also be defractionalized in time if other factors remained constant. The proximal effect of electoral systems, in the redistribution of competitive advantage after a single election, is systematically biased toward defractionalization. A few large parties are "overpaid" in seats, while many smaller parties are "underpaid." If the future vitality of a party depends partly upon its holding legislative seats, then one would expect the overpaid large parties to get even stronger and therefore even more overpaid at later elections. And the weak, underpaid parties would be likely to become even weaker and less vital at later elections, further depressing their future representation. Hence, all else being equal, it would be predicted that elective party systems should grow progressively less fractionalized over time. The strong would grow ever stronger, the weak ever weaker.

Unfortunately for this speculation—but fortunately for the viability of liberal democracy—"all else" is neither neutral nor constant. An examination of time sequences for elective fractionalization in the twenty nations reveals no systematic trend toward defractionalized elective party competition between 1945 and 1965.[7] Eleven nations show little change in elective fractionalization, producing flat, stable curves.[8] They are Denmark, Great Britain, Iceland, Ireland, Australia, Austria, Sweden, Norway, the United States, New Zealand, and Israel. Five nations—France, Belgium, Canada, the Netherlands, and Italy—show sudden changes in fractionalization which are reversed by equally sudden changes at a later time, producing a zig-zag curve.

7. Switzerland, for which data on only one election are available, cannot be analyzed.

8. These stable situations suggest a sort of equilibrium exists in these systems between centrifugal forces and centripetal forces (including electoral systems).

Two nations—Finland and Luxembourg—show gradually increasing fractionalization over the postwar period, producing gently sloped upward curves. Only West Germany conforms to the speculation that elective fractionalization will decrease over time.

The fact that elective party systems do not usually grow less and less fractionalized over time prompts further speculation. Electoral laws act as centripetal, defractionalizing forces, advantaging large established parties and penalizing smaller "upstart" parties. But the smaller challengers continue to put up a fight, sometimes a very strong fight. And party competition does not evaporate. Two explanations appear plausible: (1) smaller parties are able to sustain their elective organization and support despite the penalties inflicted upon them by electoral laws, and (2) the centrifugal, divisive forces operating within political systems are often strong enough to supply successors to those smaller parties which are unable to sustain themselves and perish.

Both of these explanations are supported by a highly impressionistic examination of the data. Parties survive despite their being underrepresented, and new parties appear quite frequently. In Australia, the "Lang" Labor Party springs up as a reaction to the rise of the Communist party. In Canada the Cooperative Commonwealth Federation comes into being along with a dozen separatist and single-interest parties after World War II. Meanwhile, the steadily underrepresented British Liberal party and others like it elsewhere muddle through election after dismal election "wasting" most of the votes given to their candidates. The birth and survival of opposition parties is a complex process which requires detailed analysis in each country.[9] This study cannot hope to explain it.

This digression suggests a word of caution. It is clear enough that electoral systems exert genuine and systematic

9. See Robert A. Dahl, ed., *Political Oppositions in Western Democracies* (New Haven, Yale University Press, 1966).

effects upon party competition. But *elections themselves* are logically prior to the electoral laws which come into play only after the votes are in. Elections express the interplay of political forces which are enormously complicated and, of course, important. All manner of forces—social, economic, institutional, personal—express themselves in election results. Electoral laws only modify these outcomes in marginal degree:

> SIMILARITY PROPOSITION SIX: *The effect of electoral laws upon the competitive positions of political parties in legislatures is marginal by comparison to the effect of election outcomes.*

The votes received by a party predict the number of seats it will hold more accurately than do the provisions of any election law. Of course, as the foregoing analysis has demonstrated, electoral laws deflect these predictions, but they do so only marginally. Consider Figure 4.3, which is a frequency polygon for the average deviations of party seat shares from the vote shares of the same parties. This average deviation, noted by the letter I, is the average of the deviations of vote and seat shares for all parties contesting an election:[10]

$$I = \frac{|T_a - S_a| + |T_r - S_r| + |T_i - S_i| \ldots + |T_n - S_n|}{n}$$

or,

$$I = \sum_{i=1}^{n} \frac{|T_i - S_i|}{N}$$

Figure 4.3 shows that the average of these average deviations (I) for the 116 elections is only 2.39 per cent or a proportion of 0.239. And proportions above 5 per cent are

10. These deviations are summed in absolute numbers, so that minus and plus differences are counted positively together. Parties whose shares of the vote are less than one-half per cent are excluded from this computation.

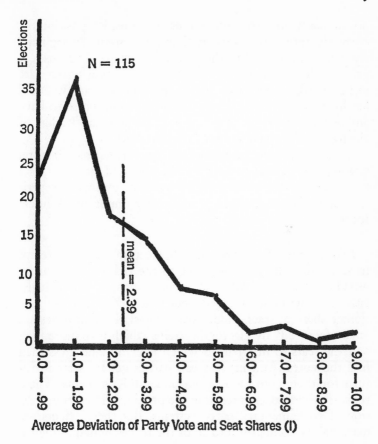

Figure 4.3
AVERAGE DEVIATION OF VOTE AND SEAT
SHARES AS PER CENTS

quite rare, since the distribution is skewed toward proportionality (I = o). This extreme, perfect proportionality is
never actualized, but it is approached by a number of
(P.R.) systems.

The implication of these data is that electoral systems do

not *radically* alter the outcome of elections. Proposition Six correctly terms the effect of electoral systems "marginal." By comparison to all of the forces that shape elections, expressing themselves in the vote returns, electoral systems are rather weak. And, from a political perspective, it could hardly be otherwise, because elections would cease to have any effect upon the choice of governmental leaders if electoral laws utterly jumbled the outcomes.

This should not be interpreted to mean that electoral systems are inconsequential to the electoral process. As I have suggested at several junctures, the systematic repetition of marginal effects is a potentially important political force.

* * *

Like the Sheriff of Nottingham, electoral systems are apt to steal from the poor and give to the rich: strong parties usually obtain more than their proportionate share of legislative seats while weak parties receive less than their proportionate share of seats. Indeed many legislative majorities are "manufactured" by electoral systems which give more than half the seats to first parties which have obtained less than half the votes. And many weak parties get *no* seats in return for their vote totals, even under P.R. systems. These redistributive patterns result in the proximal defractionalization of parliamentary party systems. But these effects are marginal by comparison to all of the forces which influence the election outcomes themselves.

If most electoral systems share the same *directional* pattern of redistribution, there are still very important differences in the *strength* or *degree* of this pattern. The next four chapters analyze some of these differences.

CHAPTER 5

DIFFERENCES BETWEEN PROPORTIONAL REPRESENTATION AND FIRST-PAST-THE-POST FORMULAE

The main lesson of the analysis reported in Chapter 4 is that most electoral systems exert similar effects upon party competition most of the time. As a rule strong parties profit at the expense of weak parties; the strong*est* parties usually receive especially favorable treatment, sometimes even obtaining unearned legislative majorities; the weakest (electoral parties are often denied parliamentary representation; and, through the interaction of all these factors, legislative party systems are usually defractionalized. But the data also show considerable variation within the limits of these generalizations, and in this chapter one aspect of that variation is analyzed. It will be well to remember that differences typically involve degrees, not directions. If, for example, all electoral systems work to the advantage of leading parties, the problem for analysis is obviously not to identify which electoral systems have that effect, but to differentiate the degrees to which various systems benefit the leading parties. That expectation guides the analysis of variation presented in this chapter and those which follow.

The differential effects of *electoral formulae* can be examined at two main levels of generality. First, the effects of majority and plurality formulae can be differentiated from the effects of proportional representation formulae. But since these two classes are far from homogeneous, it will also be interesting to analyze the differing effects of sub-types within the majority-plurality group and within the proportional representation group. These secondary comparisons distinguish between plurality formulae and their majoritarian kin, and between P.R. formulae based on "highest averages" procedures and those which follow "largest remainder" procedures. Let us begin with the first level of analysis, depending on the second level to explain some of the "loose ends" which the first leaves.

Plurality-Majority Formulae Compared with Proportional Formulae

If, as we already know, most electoral formulae have a number of effects in common, it also is clear that these effects are stronger under plurality and majority formulae than under P.R. formulae. Proportional representation tends, in effect, to mitigate the apparent biases of majority and plurality formulae, but it does not eliminate or reverse them. The generalizations presented here are meant to describe the extent of these differentials.

Proposition One in the last chapter showed that virtually all electoral systems work to the disadvantage of weak parties. The stronger parties usually receive more than proportional shares of seats while weaker parties obtain less than proportionate shares. The extent of this bias varies with electoral formulae:

DIFFERENTIAL PROPOSITION ONE: *The relative advantage of strong elective parties over weak ones found in all electoral systems tends to be greater under plurality or majority formulae than under proportional representation formulae.*

If this proposition is correct, the "bonuses" of seats given strong parties and the penalties imposed upon weak ones will be greater under plurality-majority formulae, and smaller under P.R. formulae. An examination of the relationships between vote shares (T) and seat shares (S) for strong and weak parties under the two groups of formulae will allow me to test this prediction. This is accomplished by two scattergrams, one for plurality-majority and one for P.R. formulae, both shown in Figure 5.1. If there were no systematic difference between the two groups of formulae in this respect, the regression of seat shares (S) against vote shares (T) would be the same for both scattergrams, which is not the case.

Under proportional representation formulae, the regression of seat shares against vote shares is expressed by the least-squares formula:

$$S = 1.07\,T - 0.0084$$

As vote shares are increased, seat shares increase at a slightly greater rate: a unit of increment in vote shares (T) produces 1.07 units of increment in seat shares (S), after an almost negligible constant has been deducted. If small parties were advantaged, this increment would be less than one unit, and if P.R. formulae produced full equity between large and small competitors, the increment would be exactly one unit. The conclusion to which the actual regression leads us is that P.R. formulae tend to give a *small advantage* to the strong parties over the weak ones in the apportionment of legislative seats.

Under majority and plurality formulae, the regression of seat shares against vote shares is expressed by the formula:

$$S = 1.20\,T - 0.063$$

This is a steeper slope than was found under P.R. formulae: under majority and plurality systems, a unit's increase in vote shares (T) produces 1.20 units increase in seat shares (S) after a constant of 0.063 units is deducted. This notice-

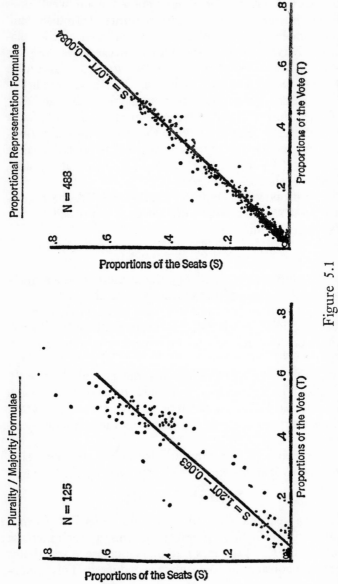

Figure 5.1

PROPORTIONS OF THE SEATS (S) PLOTTED AGAINST PROPORTIONS OF THE VOTE (T): PLURALITY–MAJORITY FORMULAE COMPARED WITH PROPORTIONAL REPRESENTATION

ably steeper slope suggests that plurality and majority formulae give a greater advantage to large elective parties over small ones than do P.R. formulae. Both groups of formulae are apt to award more than proportionate shares of seats to strong parties and less than proportionate shares to the weaker ones, but this bias is considerably more pronounced under plurality-majority formulae than under P.R. formulae. Differential Proposition One is correct.[1]

From this, it would seem to follow that the advantage given to the strongest single party in elections conducted under plurality-majority formulae is apt to be greater than the advantage given this leading party under proportional representation formulae. Since Proposition Two in the last chapter showed that almost all electoral systems advantage these leading elective parties in the allocation of legislative seats, this difference will be a matter of degree:

> DIFFERENTIAL PROPOSITION TWO: *Plurality and majority formulae tend to give a greater advantage to first parties than do proportional representation formulae.*[2]

If this proposition is correct, it follows that the bonuses of seats obtained by leading parties will tend to be greater under plurality-majority formulae than under P.R. formulae. For any one election under either type of formulae, this bonus may be defined:

$$P_p - P_e$$

This subtraction tells us how much greater the leading party's share of the seats (P_p) was than its share of the votes (P_e). The average size of this bonus will reflect the differential tendency predicted by the proposition, if it in fact exists. And the difference of the mean bonuses under the two formulae is considerable. P.R. formulae award an aver-

1. This finding is implicit in many previous discussions of electoral formulae, notably Duverger's *Political Parties*.
2. "First party" denotes the party which polled the largest single share of the vote (i.e a popular plurality).

age bonus of only 1.24 per cent, while first-past-the-post formulae award an average bonus of 8.12 per cent. This is a sixfold difference.

Clearly, Differential Proposition Two is confirmed by these findings: the bonus given leading parties under plurality-majority formulae is, on the average, greater than the bonus given them under proportional representation. Indeed, the average bonus is about six and one-half times as great under plurality or majority formulae. This difference accounts for the somewhat greater frequency with which what I have called "manufactured majorities" occur under plurality formulae (Proposition Three, Chapter 4).

About the same pattern occurs with respect to the collective fate of the two strongest parties: plurality-majority formulae give an average bonus of 5.46 per cent to the first two parties, while P.R. formulae award them an average bonus of 2.90 per cent of the total seats. The plurality-majority figure is lower for the first two parties than for the first party, largely because part of the large bonus given first parties is taken away from the second party in two-party systems. The implication of these findings, well known to the scholarly literature, is that single-member plurality systems may cause the development and maintenance of two-party systems. Maurice Duverger's is perhaps the best-known formulation of this hypothesis:

> *The simple-majority* [plurality] *single-ballot system favors the two-party system.* Of all the hypotheses that have been defined in this book, this approaches the most nearly perhaps to a true sociological law. An almost complete correlation is observable between the simple-majority single-ballot system and the two-party system: dualist countries use the simple-majority vote and simple-majority vote countries are dualist. The exceptions are very rare and can generally be explained as a result of special conditions.[3]

3. Duverger, p. 217 (italics in original).

Let us restate this hypothesis as follows:

PROVISIONAL DIFFERENTIAL PROPOSITION THREE: *Plurality formulae cause two-party systems.*

This proposition implies that plurality formulae are a necessary and sufficient condition for two-party competition. If this is correct for the twenty nations analyzed here, all two-party systems will be associated with plurality formulae, and all plurality formulae will be associated with two-party systems. By the same logic, no other formulae will be associated with two-party competition, and two-party systems will never exist beside formulae other than plurality types.[4] If these conditions obtain, all cases will be concentrated in the upper left and lower right cells of Table 5.1

TABLE 5.1
TWO-PARTY SYSTEMS * AS A FUNCTION
OF PLURALITY FORMULAE

$N = 107$

FORMULAE

	Plurality	Other	
Two-Party	23	4	
			$\lambda_a = 0.59$
Other	7	73	

PARTY SYSTEMS

* Two-party systems are defined as those in which the first party holds less than 70% of the legislative seats, and the first two parties together hold at least 90% of the seats: $P_p = .70$ and $W_p = .90$. N is only 107 because eight Australian elections are excluded.

below, indicating a perfect correlation between two-party systems and plurality formulae.

4. The Australian case of majority, single-member voting is put aside temporarily, because its majority formula, combined with single-member districting, adds an unnecessary ambiguity to this analysis.

Of the 107 cases, 89.7 per cent fall into the predicted categories of association: plurality formulae with two-party systems and other formulae with other party systems.[5] This suggests a relationship which is somewhat weaker than the term "sociological law" might lead one to expect, but it is, nevertheless, a strong association. In light of the many other sources of variation likely to impinge upon the nature of party competition, the statistical data are indeed impressive. It may be useful to examine the eleven exceptional cases.

Seven plurality elections failed to produce two-party legislative competition, and all of them were Canadian. In six, the two strongest parties failed to obtain 90 per cent of the seats, and in one, the first party obtained 78 per cent of the seats, suggesting something closer to one-party competition. The Canadian exceptions have a fairly obvious explanation: the intense hostility between overlapping regional, cultural, and linguistic groups produced a strong base of support for locally strong minority parties. In some districts, many of them in Quebec, Progressive Conservative and Liberal candidates are defeated by the candidates of locally popular minor parties such as Social Credit and various French separatist parties. This happened in about 15 per cent of the Dominion's parliamentary districts in most of the postwar elections. I pointed out in Chapter 4 that these small Canadian parties were often heavily underrepresented, but an examination of the data in time sequence shows no trend toward their demise. If anything, they grew a little stronger during the late 1950s and early 1960s. It must be conceded that the Canadian exception is a valid and important one, which necessitates modification of the proposition that plurality formulae cause two-party competition.

5. Guttman's Coefficient of Predictability (λ_a) produces a value of 0.59 for electoral systems as predictors of party systems. For the two-way association, it produces a value of 0.61. In short, this is a strong, though imperfect association. The value of Lambda compensates for the imbalance of the marginal totals, as the simple percentage does not.

Four Austrian elections were exceptional in an opposite sense: P.R. produced two-party legislative competition, or, until recently, legislative collaboration between the two major parties, the conservative People's Party and the Socialists. In the four elections, the total seat shares of the minor parties amounted to less than 10 per cent. The sources of this unusual association between a P.R. formula and two-party competition are no doubt complex, and would require detailed research if a full explanation were desired. For some reason, Austrian politics failed to generate small parties capable of winning important shares of parliamentary representation. Typically, these small parties received only about 10 per cent of the popular vote and only 5 per cent of the seats. While the electoral system—d'Hondt highest average formula, party list ballots, and rather small, complex districts averaging only 5.7 seats each—did impose a considerable penalty upon them, this does not altogether explain their collective weakness in the popular vote. Apparently, divisive political forces were too few and too weak to sustain these elective parties.

Together, the Canadian and Austrian exceptions suggest that the proposition requires revision. Plurality formulae were not altogether sufficient conditions for two-party competition in Canada, and they were not necessary conditions to two-party competition in Austria. A simple causal explanation must accordingly be discarded. Yet these exceptions must not be given so much emphasis that they distract us from the very strong relationship observed in the other countries. Perhaps an accurate assessment is offered by a revised proposition:

DIFFERENTIAL PROPOSITION THREE: *Plurality formulae are always associated with two-party competition except where strong local minority parties exist, and other formulae are associated with two-party competition only where minority elective parties are very weak.*

This is of course a much less dramatic proposition than the one with which we began. It recognizes the importance of other factors within political systems which compete with electoral formulae for control of party competition. This is another occasion which suggests that the influence of electoral laws upon legislative party systems is usually less important than the many forces expressed in election outcomes.[6] That, of course, is no surprise to anyone, least of all the student of elections.

Another interesting question concerns the extent to which P.R. and other formulae produce the proportional outcomes which the former are designed to produce. Does P.R. decrease the deviation between party shares of the vote and seats as advertised?

DIFFERENTIAL PROPOSITION FOUR: *Proportional representation formulae tend to allocate seats more proportionally than do majority and plurality formulae.*

This hypothesis suggests that the average deviation between each party's share of the vote and its share of the seats in each election (I) will be lower under P.R. formulae than it is under majority and plurality formulae. In 71 P.R. elections, the average deviation was 1.63 per cent of the total seats, meaning that, on the average, each party's share of the seats deviated by only 1.63 per cent from its share in the popular vote. The average deviation found in 39 non-P.R. elections was 3.96 per cent of the total seats, meaning that the average deviation was more than twice as great under these majority and plurality formulae.[7]

6. Furthermore, it is not possible to distinguish between the effects of plurality formulae and the single-member districts with which they are always associated.

7. Unfortunately, it is not possible to determine the extent to which district magnitudes, not electoral formulae, are responsible for the differences. It seems likely that single-member districts account for most of the difference, due to the dependence of outcomes on geographic distribution of the vote under such districts. See Schattschneider, *Party Government*, p. 70.

It may be concluded that the proposition is correct, but that the difference is a matter of degree and not direction. And there are a number of exceptional cases. The 1954 election for the United States House of Representatives, conducted without the benefit of proportional representation, produced an average deviation of only 0.57 per cent of the total seats. One Icelandic election, conducted before the reform of 1959 but under a form of P.R., yielded an average deviation of 7.24 per cent of the total seats. It must be concluded that, from the proportionalist perspective, P.R. is not a complete solution to the evil of electoral injustice, and that plurality elections do not always produce great injustices. But, on the whole, P.R. formulae are more likely than others to achieve their intended purpose—proportional allocation of legislative seats.

The burden of the less proportional results obtained under majority and plurality formulae falls heavily upon the weakest elective parties:

DIFFERENTIAL PROPOSITION FIVE: *Plurality and majority formulae tend to deny representation to larger numbers of small parties than proportional representation formulae.*

Plurality and majority formulae in 39 elections exclude an average of 2.34 weak parties from parliament, but P.R. formulae in 71 elections denied representation to an average of only 0.79 weak parties. This less charitable attitude toward weak competitors is greatest under single-member systems (the Australian majority formula and the other plurality formulae) in elections where many small parties nominated candidates. It was not intense under the French double-ballot system. It is, however, clear that the proposition is generally correct.

It would seem to follow from all of the foregoing differences that plurality and majority systems are usually associated with less fractionalized party systems, both elective and parliamentary:

> DIFFERENTIAL PROPOSITION SIX: *P.R. electoral systems tend to be associated with more fractionalized elective and parliamentary party systems than plurality and majority formulae.*

Fractionalization values, both elective and parliamentary, are higher for most P.R. elections than for plurality and majority elections. While there is some overlapping, the central tendencies are obvious enough. The average fractionalization value for P.R. elective party systems (F_e) is 0.73; the average for plurality and majority systems is only 0.54. The average fractionalization of legislative party systems (F_p) under P.R. is 0.70, but the same average under other formulae is only 0.51. Another way to state this obvious difference is to say that multipartism is more common and more extreme under proportional representation than under first-past-the-post systems.

Does this difference have any significance for legislative politics? The answer is clearly affirmative! Most of the political systems analyzed in this study are parliamentary regimes, in which the government can be stable only with a majority of legislators supporting it.[8] Certainly, the relative ease or difficulty with which majority support can be pieced together depends in part upon the degree to which the parliamentary party system is fractionalized. If a few large legislative parties monopolize the chamber, it should generally be easier to sustain a government than if the body is fractionalized into a large number of small parties. Other factors—notably the willingness of party leaders to enter and sustain coalitions with each other—will also be very important, but the base line from which majority building

8. The United States is the only clear exception to this generalization.

begins is the distribution of legislative seats among the parties. And this is, of course, the variable which I have been analyzing.

The minimum majority in a legislature[9]—the smallest number of parties which can combine to form a majority assuming full willingness to enter coalitions—depends upon the extent to which legislative parties are fractionalized. With defractionalized parliamentary party systems, fewer parties are required, and indeed a single party may hold a majority of its own. But with highly fractionalized party systems, many parties must combine if a working majority is to be obtained by the resulting government. P.R. formulae are associated with greater fractionalization, both elective and legislative. Hence:

DIFFERENTIAL PROPOSITION SEVEN: *Minimal legislative majorities will tend to be larger in bodies elected under P.R. formulae, and smaller in bodies elected under plurality or majority formulae.*

The data confirm the proposition. In 75 legislatures elected under P.R. formulae, the mean minimal majority was 1.96 parties. Typically, the support of the two largest parties was required for the formation of a majority. In 45 legislatures elected under majority and plurality formulae, the mean minimal majority was only 1.15 parties, suggesting that one-party majorities were more common, and that "big party–small party" coalitions were often sufficient in their absence. A more detailed analysis of British, Canadian, American, Australian, and New Zealander legislative party systems would demonstrate the validity of this finding. The Fifth Republic's French National Assemblies, elected under the double ballot plurality-majority formula, constitute the only deviant cases. In short, the hypothesis appears to be

9. For an operational definition, see Chapter 3 above.

sustained by the data, and governments are more simply
supported by the parliaments of plurality or majority systems than they are by those of P.R. systems.[10]

One more important difference between P.R. and other
formulae remains. An important component of democratic
party politics is legitimate *change*,[11] and the history of a
political system turns in part upon the changing fortunes of
its political parties. Certainly, the rise of the British Labor
party in the 1920s and the corresponding demise of the British Liberals were among the crucial events of that nation's
recent history. The same could be said about the decline of
French Radicalism after World War II; the long famine
of the American Republicans precipitated by the Great
Depression and Franklin Roosevelt; or, perhaps, the recent
defeat of the Norwegian Labor party. Changes of this kind
both record and implement major changes in the political
systems of democratic nations.

Since we have already seen that electoral formulae are
not neutral in other important respects, it might be expected
that they would exert an influence upon the rapidity with
which party fortunes reverse themselves. Some formulae
might mask changes in the relative strength of parties, while
others might exaggerate these changes. Under one formula,
a gain or loss of 10 per cent in popular support might be
reflected in a change of 30 per cent in parliamentary representation, but it might be covered up by another formula.
In fact, it appears that no electoral systems have this damp-
ing effect upon changes in party strength, and that all of

10. It would be interesting to analyze the relationship between minimal
majorities and a number of other variables such as government stability,
immobilisme, and the legitimacy of parliamentary institutions. Unfortunately, that analysis would require a study at least as wide in scope as
this one, so I cannot pursue it here. A superficial discussion of selected
cases would add to the literary interest of this study, but would also de-
tract from its scientific interest, since the selection would necessarily be
arbitrary.

11. Thomas Landon Thorson's *The Logic of Democracy* (New York,
Holt, Rinehart and Winston, 1962) suggests that the legitimately open
possibility of change is the distinguishing virtue of democracy.

them are apt to either exert a neutral effect or to magnify such changes. To speak formally:

DIFFERENTIAL PROPOSITION EIGHT: *Plurality and majority formulae tend to magnify changes in the popular support of parties when legislative seats are allocated, but P.R. systems generally have no such effect.*

An analysis of changes in shares of the vote and shares of the seats for the parties with 2 per cent or more of the vote confirms this hypothesis.[12] The average change of party vote shares from one election to the next (E_e) may be compared with average changes in seat shares for the same parties (E_p). If the two averages are about the same, no magnification of changing party fortunes has occurred; if legislative changes (E_p) exceed elective changes (E_e), then some such magnification has occurred. Table 5.2 shows

TABLE 5.2
CHANGES IN VOTE AND SEAT SHARES *

	Average changes in vote shares (E_e)	Average changes in seat shares (E_p)	Net average magnification of changing party strength
P.R. Formulae N = 55	2.58%	2.68%	0.10%
Plurality Majority Formulae N = 30	3.24%	6.86%	3.62%

* The figures are expressed as per cents of total seats. Some elections are excluded from this analysis because of changing party labels, and the first postwar election for each nation is excluded for want of comparative data on the last previous election.

these comparisons for elections decided by P.R. formulae and for elections decided otherwise.

12. For an operational definition of the variable used here, see Chapter 3.

On the average, P.R. systems produced no meaningful magnification, and an examination of the actual data suggests that this was an almost uniform pattern throughout the period for all of the P.R. systems. In sharp contrast, plurality and majority systems tended to magnify changes in party strength twofold. That is, a party's increase in vote share was typically doubled in its seat share, and its loss in vote shares was doubly reflected in its seat share. Hence, the effects of changing popular support were magnified by these electoral formulae, but were not magnified by P.R. formulae.

The tendency of majority or plurality formulae—always associated with single-member districts—to magnify the changing fortunes of political parties in legislatures requires explanation. The crucial event appears to hinge upon the single-member district itself, and, more specifically, upon the *marginal single-member district*. The Second Congressional District in the State of Oregon provides a good illustration of the magnification produced by these marginal districts. This rural district, comprising the eastern two thirds of the state, normally returns about 90,000 votes. In 1954, the Republican candidate won by 4,256 votes, and in 1956 the Democrats took the seat by 1,375 votes.[13] A change of less than 5 per cent of the popular vote has produced a 100 per cent reversal in the control of the district's seat in Washington. This is an enormous magnification of the change that actually occurred in the relative strength of the two elective parties. Many such changes will cancel each other out when all of a legislature's districts are considered, but the very strength of the district magnification, coupled with the probability of national, inter-district trends in voting explain the net magnification.

The theoretical implication of this generalization is ironic.

13. See U.S., Bureau of the Census, *Congressional District Data Book* (*Districts of the 88th Congress*), A Statistical Abstract Supplement (Washington, U.S. Government Printing Office, 1963), p. 415.

First-past-the-post formulae are a conservative force in their effect upon the relationship between large established parties and small challengers. They tend to maintain the status quo by protecting these established parties from minor party competition. P.R. systems are not so conservative in that connection. But, with respect to relationships *between* the established parties, first-past-the-post formulae appear to be radical agencies, since they exaggerate the effects of changes in the relative strength of these parties. In this connection, P.R. formulae are not positively conservative, but are certainly less radical than the plurality and majority formulae.

* * *

The redistributive effects attributed to electoral systems in general are usually most intense under first-past-the-post formulae and least intense under P.R. formulae. The former are apt to give a greater advantage to strong parties, especially the strong*est* parties, and to exclude more weak parties from representation. And these formulae seem to magnify changes in the popular support of the parties, while P.R. formulae do not appreciably magnify such changes.

First-past-the-post formulae cannot be said to cause the genesis or maintenance of two-party systems, although there is a strong statistical association between the two. P.R. formulae are associated with more fractionalized party systems, but cannot be said to cause them. And, of course, P.R. formulae are associated with more proportional seat allocations. None of them, however, produces perfectly proportional allocations.

In this analysis, a number of specific electoral formulae have been put aside, and the next chapter is given over to their analysis.

CHAPTER 6

SOME MORE SPECIFIC TYPES
OF ELECTORAL FORMULAE

In Chapter 5 two broad classes of electoral formulae—proportional representation and first-past-the-post—were differentiated by their effects upon party systems. But, since these two classes are quite heterogeneous, it is also of interest to make specific comparisons between subtypes. First, "highest average" and "largest remainder" procedures for proportional representation are compared. Second, majority formulae are distinguished from their plurality relatives. And third, two unusual formulae—the Irish and West German—are analyzed individually.

Highest Average and Largest
Remainder Procedures Compared

The properties which earlier analysis ascribed to P.R. formulae are found in their purest, most intense versions where largest remainder formulae are employed—Italy, Luxembourg, and, since 1951, Israel. And these effects are somewhat less pronounced in electoral systems that rest upon the highest average procedure.[1] At base, the reason

1. Nations using highest average P.R. formulae are Austria, Belgium, Finland, Israel (pre-1951), Sweden, Norway, and Switzerland.

of these differentials accurately describes the variation of mean quantities. If the mean reflects the general pattern—as indeed it does—then it is reasonable to conclude that Differential Proposition Eleven is correct.[2]

What significance may be attached to these differentials? In a causal sense, almost none, since we have no way to analyze intervening variables of obvious importance. But from the normative perspectives which have been so important in the literature on electoral laws, some significance may be attached to the difference between largest remainder and highest average formulae. First, largest remainder formulae appear to conform more closely to the stringent requirements of the proportionalist position than do highest average formulae. Second, highest average formulae seem more useful if one entertains the pragmatic value of simplifying party choices to fewer, more powerful alternatives. And third, it should be noticed the differentials between these subtypes of P.R. are less intense than the differentials between P.R. generally and the first-past-the-post formulae.

Majority Formulae

Among the twenty countries analyzed in this study, only two use majority formulae—France and Australia. Neither can be compared simply with plurality formulae, since both are linked with an important intervening institutional factor. In France, the intervening factor is the double-ballot, and in Australia, it is the alternative-vote ballot. Like plurality formulae, however, both use single-member districts. These considerations suggest that the French and Australian formulae should be considered singly.

The Australian Majority Formula[3]

An earlier analysis, reported in Chapter 5 above, showed

2. In less explicit form, the differentials found here are suggested by Mackenzie, *Free Elections*, pp. 79–80.

3. The Australian formula is also known as the "Ware System." See van den Bergh, *Unity in Diversity*, pp. 6–7.

that the Australian majority formula was associated with two-party competition, and that association was attributed to the single-member district system. It is appropriate here to say simply that the Australian system behaves in all its particulars as if it were a single-member district plurality formula.

> SIMILARITY PROPOSITION SEVEN: *All of the properties associated with plurality formulae are also associated with the Australian majority formula.*

An analysis of the data substantiates this generalization. Values for fractionalization, deviation of vote and seat shares, the numbers of elective and parliamentary parties, the strength of the first party and the first two parties, and the data for the magnification of changes in elective strength all suggest that the Australian formula behaves like an ordinary plurality formula. Indeed the data show no pattern for Australia which is in the least untypical of plurality systems taken as a whole.[4]

This suggests that the single-member district is the critical property in both types of formulae, which accounts for their shared effects. For a further analysis of single-member districts, the reader is referred to Chapter 7 below.

The French Majority-Plurality Formula[5]

When General de Gaulle and his followers came to power in the crisis of 1958, one of the reforms they instituted was a return to the double-ballot system of the Third Republic. This system was imposed upon the highly fractionalized party system which had existed under the Fourth Republic, and it coincided with the rise of the U.N.R. (Gaullist) party. This coincidence, compounded by the

4. See Chapter 2 for a description of this system.
5. Since vote totals included second and third choices actually counted, but not those "wasted," these data are not strictly comparable with data for systems with simple (not alternative) voting.

general instability of French politics in that period, makes it very difficult to draw reliable conclusions about the effect of the new electoral law. Accordingly, no attempt will be made to generalize these findings. This is simply a description of what happened under the double-ballot majority-plurality formula in the first two Fifth Republic elections. The most salient observations are these:

1. The majority-plurality formula produced highly disproportional results, with average deviations of vote and seat shares running 7.49 per cent and 5.08 per cent in the two elections.

2. These disproportions worked to the advantage of the first party (the U.N.R.), which received bonuses in seats of 20.4 per cent and 17.4 per cent of the total seats in the two elections. These are quite extraordinary, even by plurality formula standards.

3. Both elections produced minimal majorities of two parties.

4. Both elections exerted strong defractionalizing effects upon the legislative party systems.

These findings are not consistent with Maurice Duverger's generalization about the double-ballot, majority-plurality formula. According to Duverger, "the majority system with two ballots encourages a system of parties that are multiple." [6] If anything at all can be said about the above generalizations, it is that they suggest a defractionalizing trend, working to the advantage of fewer, larger parties, and against the multi-party system predicted by Duverger. The extreme of two-party competition is not reached, or even approached, but the effects of the electoral system appear to tend in that direction, and certainly do not suggest the encouragement of many small parties. What is to be made of this apparent contradiction?

I suggest that the two-ballot formula is causally related

6. Duverger, p. 205.

to multi-partism only if two other conditions are also met: (1) there must be no party which is capable of winning pluralities or majorities in a large number of districts without the cooperation of other parties, and (2) there must be a number of relatively small parties which are willing and able to "trade districts" on the second ballot to assure representation to all.[7] District trading means that the parties withdraw candidates to advantage each other's candidates on a reciprocal basis. Since the available data are drawn from a short, probably atypical period, I will resist the temptation to claim more than speculative validity for these suggestions.

From this brief analysis of the French and Australian cases, it must be concluded that the majority formula cannot be regarded as a homogeneous class, with properties of its own. For reasons explained in Chapter 2 the majority formula never appears in unalloyed form, and even after being combined with "softening" institutions which prevent electoral deadlock it is rarely used for elections. Its effects cannot be delineated in systematic form, and this brief discussion must end without an attempt at broad-gauge generalization. No general patterns are to be found.

Two Unusual Formulae

The formulae used to elect the Irish Dail and the West German *Bundestag* are so unusual and so significant that they require separate examination.

The Irish Hare Formula

After winning their independence, the Irish could hardly have been expected to adopt an electoral law which smacked of the English heritage. In fact, they adopted a law originated by a British lawyer, Thomas Hare, in the mid-nineteenth century, and advocated by John Stuart Mill.

7. See Roy C. Macridis and Robert E. Ward, eds., *Modern Political Systems—Europe* (Englewood Cliffs, Prentice-Hall, 1963), p. 220.

The modified version of Hare's scheme of vote transference is described in Chapter 2; here I examine its specific effects upon party competition.

In general, the Irish formula behaves like any other sort of proportional representation. It operates quite proportionally, producing an average vote-seat deviation of only 1.51 per cent of the total seats. It excludes very few electoral parties from the Dail. It is associated with fractionalized multi-party competition. But it exerts a modest defractionalizing effect upon legislative parties; the average F value for elections is 0.70, but only 0.66 for legislative seats. With one exception, it has consistently produced minimal majorities of two Dail parties. It awards a modest bonus of 2 per cent to 5 per cent to the strongest elective party, and a slightly larger bonus of 2 per cent to 7 per cent to the two strongest parties together. It is, however, difficult to evaluate these data because the vote totals include second and third choices which were eventually counted under the complicated Hare procedure, but do not include the residual returns never counted. It may well mask certain deviations, and the surface relationships reported here may, therefore, be less constant than they seem.

This electoral formula, widely hailed by proportionalists as the leading living example of electoral justice, is perhaps a bit too involuted for the taste of men who run for the Dail. In 1958, in fact, the Dail passed a reform bill which would have substituted a single-member plurality system for the Hare system. Fortunately for the pride of proportionalists, the Irish voters were well enough pleased with the Hare formula to vote down the referendum on the reform bill when it was submitted to them a year later.[8]

The German Plurality-Proportionality Formula

The German formula, twice reformed during the period

8. See Basel Chubb, "Ireland 1957," in *Elections Abroad*, ed. David E. Butler (London, Macmillan, 1959), p. 183.

studied, is an almost complete hybrid of P.R. and first-past-the-post formulae. For a description of the law's content, the reader may turn back to Chapter I. The question which interests me here is, "Does the formula behave more like P.R. or plurality?"

In some ways, the German hybrid formula operates very much like a P.R. formula. The average vote-seat deviation is only 1.37 per cent, which is a little lower than the average deviation of P.R. formulae in general. While elective fractionalization shows a downward trend over the twenty years, the total average for elective fractionalization is 0.73 units, about that of P.R. formulae in general (0.73 units). It awards a moderate average bonus of 3.5 per cent to the leading elective party (CDU/CSU). In all of these respects, the German hybrid could pass as a P.R. formula.

Yet there is a sense in which the formula's effects approximate a plurality formula: the formula exerts a strong defractionalizing effect upon legislative parties. Elective fractionalization averages 0.73 units, while legislative fractionalization averages only 0.66 units. This effect is about twice as great as the norm for P.R. formulae, and is actually greater than the normal effect of plurality formulae. Most of this very considerable defractionalization is explained by the formula's tendency to deny representation to a large number of weak elective parties. On the average, 4.5 such parties have been excluded from the *Bundestag*. Why? Because the P.R. provisions of the law are applied only to those parties which win a minimum number of plurality seats.[9] Near proportionality thus obtains for the strong parties, but a plurality effect obtains for weaker parties. Hence, the synthesis of the two formulae breaks down with the strength of elective parties; for all practical purposes, weak parties confront a plurality formula.

9. This minimum has varied during the period but it has entailed three basic standards: (1) 5% of the vote in each *länder*, (2) 5% of the national vote, and (3) three single-member district pluralities. These are obviously harsh standards for small parties.

All of this is a drastic simplification of the reality of party competition under this unusual formula. Fortunately, an excellent study is available, in Uwe Kitzinger's *German Electoral Politics*.

The findings reported in this chapter form no general pattern. In effect, I have identified and analyzed a number of "special cases," which diverge in some important respects from the more general classes of electoral formulae analyzed earlier. Briefly, the findings of these specialized analyses are as follows:

1. Largest remainder formulae produce more proportional results than do highest average formulae, and the effects associated with P.R. are therefore more pronounced under largest remainder than under highest average formulae (Differential Proposition Eleven).
2. The Australian "Ware" majority formula appears to operate very much as if it were a plurality formula, and this similarity appears to follow from Australia's single-member districts.
3. The French Fifth Republic's majority-plurality formula does not appear to foster multi-partism, but the data are too limited to allow generalizations beyond that negative finding.
4. The Irish Hare formula appears to operate like a party-list P.R. formula.
5. The German plurality-proportionality formula appears to behave like a P.R. formula with respect to strong elective parties, but to impose a harsh plurality-like penalty upon weak elective parties.

These findings contribute no reliable, general propositions to our knowledge of electoral politics, but are of some interest as descriptive generalizations pertaining to single nations, or small groups of nations. On this timid note, my analysis of electoral formulae ends; district magnitudes become the focal variables of analysis in the next chapter.

CHAPTER 7

DISTRICT MAGNITUDE, PROPORTIONALITY, AND PARTY COMPETITION

District Magnitudes

Electoral formulae allocate legislative seats within electoral districts. If these districts contain only a single seat, no electoral formula can be expected to produce a proportional allocation of seats among the competing parties, because it can reward only one party with a seat. If the districts contain two seats, the formula may produce a more nearly proportional result, but cannot be expected to approach perfect proportionality unless the voters are kind enough to cast their votes in fractions with divisors of two. As the number of seats in each district increases, the likelihood that any given formula will approximate proportionality also increases, because the larger number of available seats introduces a more flexible combination of rewards with which to account for the relative voting strength of the parties. The average number of seats allocated in each electoral district, a quantity which I have labeled "district magnitude" (M), may therefore exert an important impact upon the relative proportionality of electoral systems. And if that is so, it follows that competitive relationships between parties are also likely to be influenced by district magnitudes. James Hogan has stated these speculations quite nicely:

> the decisive point in P.R. is the size of the constituencies: the larger the constituencies, that is, the greater the number of members which it elects, the more closely will the result approximate proportionality. On the other hand, the smaller the constituency, that is, the fewer the number of members which it returns, the more radical will be the departure from proportionality . . . the proportionality system in so far as it conforms to the principle of proportionality makes for [party] multiplication.[1]

It is the task of this chapter to operationalize these generalizations and to test them against the available evidence, and we begin with the initial assertion that the proportionality of outcomes is a function of district magnitudes:

> DIFFERENTIAL PROPOSITION TEN: *The proportionality with which legislative seats are allocated increases in relation to the magnitude of electoral districts: the higher the magnitude, the greater the proportionality.*

Since no operational measure of proportionality itself is available, it will be useful to restate this hypothesis in negative categories:

> DIFFERENTIAL PROPOSITION TEN (*Corollary*): *The average deviation between the vote and seat shares of the parties (I) varies as an inverse proportion of district magnitude (M): as magnitudes increase, average deviations decrease.*

The average deviation of vote and seat shares (I) is an index of the disproportionate outcomes; the larger the average deviation, the less proportional the outcome. It is there-

1. Hogan, *Elections and Representation*, pp. 13, 18.

fore the opposite of proportionality, and should be inversely related to district magnitude if proportionality is positively related to magnitude. It follows that the corollary's correctness will indicate the correctness of the initial hypothesis.

Figure 7.1 shows the approximate relationship between

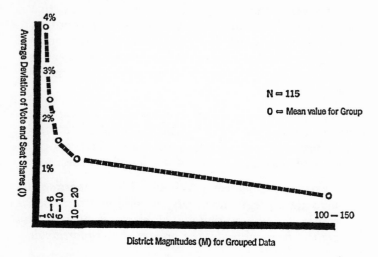

Figure 7.1

AVERAGE VOTE–SEAT DEVIATIONS (I) AS FUNCTION
OF DISTRICT MAGNITUDES (M) FOR GROUPED DATA

disproportions, given as (I) on the vertical axis, and district magnitude, given as (M) on the horizontal axis. Clearly enough, the predicted negative relationship is reflected in the trend line for the grouped data. As district magnitudes increase, disproportions decrease. Naturally, the linear correlation of these two variables (ungrouped) (M) and (I), is negative:

$$r = -0.37$$

That datum alone is sufficient to confirm the corollary,

and therefore to indicate the validity of the initial hypothesis. But a look at the trend line shown in Figure 7.1 makes it apparent that this conclusion is misleading. This is because the relationship is curvilinear:

> DIFFERENTIAL PROPOSITION ELEVEN: *The positive relationship between proportionality and district magnitude is curvilinear: as district magnitudes are increased, proportionality increases at a decreasing rate.*

Or, in its operational form:

> DIFFERENTIAL PROPOSITION ELEVEN (*Corollary*): *The negative relationship between average vote-seat deviations (I) and district magnitude (M) is curvilinear: as district magnitudes are increased, deviations between vote and seat shares decrease at a decreasing rate.*

In practical terms, this means that an increase in district magnitudes will reduce the disproportions of election outcomes, but that the decrease will become proportionately less as initial magnitudes increase. For district magnitudes of twenty or less, the curve for the grouped data is approximated by the formula:

$$I = \frac{12}{M}$$

In this zone, shown at the left in Figure 7.1, the increasing proportionality associated with the addition of each new seat to district magnitude is considerable. The difference between single-member districts (M = 1), and small multi-member districts (M = 2 to 6) is great, since average deviations decline by more than one third of the total in that zone. Up to magnitudes of twenty, the decrease in proportionality "payoffs" is progressive, but slight. Small increases in magnitude are associated with declining but very substantial cuts in the average deviation of vote and seat shares.

When district magnitudes are raised substantially beyond

twenty, a "plateau effect" seems to take place.[2] Increasing proportionality (or decreasing deviation) appears to decline even more rapidly than the equation I have been using would suggest. Consider the data shown at the right of Figure 7.1: district magnitudes of 100 to 150 found in the Israeli and Dutch systems produce deviations which are only slightly below those found in systems with district magnitudes between ten and twenty. Unfortunately, no intermediate cases are available for analysis, so it is not possible to specify the point at which this rather sharp plateau effect begins to supplant the curve found for lower values (i.e. $I = 12/M$).

Even without being able to specify that transition point, it is possible to confirm the hypothesized curvilinear relationship: *the proportionality of outcomes increases at a decreasing rate when district magnitudes are increased.* And, of course, the disproportions between vote and seat shares decrease at a decreasing rate when district magnitudes are elevated. The *direction* of these relationships has already been explained, but one still wonders why this curvilinear relationship appears.

The data and variables employed here are not suited to causal explanation of this curvilinear relationship between proportionality and magnitude. We are dealing with mean values for an intricate process; these values are useful for plotting the gross relationship, but they are not useful for identifying the specific factors that explain the relationships which are so plotted. Such an analysis would require a district-by-district examination of both magnitude and proportionality in several systems. Accordingly, it is appropriate to limit this discussion to the descriptive generalization that magnitude is related to proportionality in curvilinear fashion.

Whatever their causes, these findings suggest an interest-

2. This analysis must be tempered to account for the long zone ($M => 20, < 100$) in which no actual cases are found.

ing problem for the electoral reformer. Suppose that the reformer seeks to optimize three values: (1) the compactness of electoral districts, (2) the smallness of the legislature elected from these districts, and (3) the proportionality of election outcomes. Increasing district magnitudes will force the reformer to sacrifice one of his first two values, because he must either (a) make the districts less compact to include more seats, or (b) leave the district compact, but add seats, thereby making the elected legislature a larger body. How far should he go with these sacrifices?

Since the proportionality added to election outcomes by each new unit of district magnitude declines as one adds to it, the reformer will confront the "law of diminishing returns." His sacrifices in district compactness and legislative size will pay their greatest dividends in proportionality when pre-reform magnitudes are small (i.e. from one to ten). More serious sacrifices, such as at-large election or enormous legislatures, will produce a poorer ratio of benefit in proportionality to cost in legislative and district size. The reformer will therefore be better advised to introduce only modest reforms if magnitude is quite low, and to find another outlet for his ambition to improve political institutions if magnitudes are already quite large (i.e. ten or more).

Another even more obvious message lies in these findings: *electoral formulae designed to produce proportionality depend in large measure upon district magnitudes for their efficacy.* Very small magnitudes of, say, three seats, will thwart even the most precise P.R. formula in its practical effect. Larger magnitudes of, say, fifteen seats, will allow even less precise P.R. formulae to approximate proportionality rather closely. Considering that formula types vary at random over the magnitudes I have been analyzing, the data substantiate these suspicions.

These findings carry important implications for party competition itself:

1. The biases of electoral systems generally tend to advantage large parties over small ones, to defractionalize legislative party systems, and therefore to restrain the multiplication of parties.

2. These biases are inversely related to proportionality: the greater the proportionality, the weaker the biases, and *vice versa.*

3. Proportionality is a curvilinear function of district magnitude.

4. It is therefore probable that the biases of electoral systems, along with their consequences for party systems, will be weakest where district magnitudes are great, and strongest where district magnitudes are low. And since the linkage (proportionality) is a curvilinear function of magnitude, it is reasonable to expect other dependent variables (the biases of electoral systems) to vary as curves with respect to district magnitudes.

As the analyses which follow will demonstrate, these deductions are mostly consistent with the facts.[3] Let me begin with a very general finding, examining specific relationships later:

> DIFFERENTIAL PROPOSITION TWELVE: *The fractionalization of party systems, both elective and legislative, varies positively with district magnitude: high magnitudes are associated with great fractionalization, and vice versa. But the relationship is curvilinear: fractionalization increases at a decreasing rate as magnitude increases.*

An examination of Table 7.1 will confirm this hypothesis. While elective fractionalization consistently exceeds legislative fractionalization, both increase at a decreasing rate with increasing district magnitudes. The increments of fraction-

3. This finding, even with the plausible supporting speculation, is not a causal theory. We can verify only the empirical pattern itself, not the speculative deductions.

alization are greatest where initial magnitudes are least, and they are least where initial magnitudes are greatest. Single-member districts, as we already know, are associated with two-party competition ($F = 0.5$), and this fact is borne out by the grouped data. The fractionalization of party systems is progressive with growing district magnitudes, but the *rate* of progression falls off steadily.

TABLE 7.1

FRACTIONALIZATION (F) AS A FUNCTION
OF DISTRICT MAGNITUDES (M)
FOR GROUPED DATA

DISTRICT MAGNITUDE	F_e	F_p
1	.548	.508
2–6	.686	.649
7–10	.718	.689
11–20	.756	.729
100–150	.785	.775

It appears that fractionalization varies about the same way proportionality does with respect to district magnitude. Fractionalization varies in a curve which is almost the opposite of the one described by vote–seat disproportions. The hypothesized relationship is therefore confirmed.

The relationship between district magnitude and party system fractionalization reported here suggests a number of more specific relationships. The analyses of these relationships, which follow, are less detailed than the above analyses because attention is given only to the direction of relationships, and not to their curvilinear properties.[4] A simplified analysis is appropriate because the remaining relationships are of less general interest.

These relationships are between more specific party system variables and district magnitude:

4. The interested reader can readily perform a graphic analysis by using the tabular data.

DIFFERENTIAL PROPOSITION THIRTEEN: *The magnitude of electoral districts (M) is positively related to:*

    a. minimal parliamentary majorities (A) entailing larger numbers of legislative parties

    b. larger numbers of elective parties (N_e)

    c. larger numbers of legislative parties (N_p)

    d. first parties which obtain smaller shares of the vote and seats (P_e and P_p)

    e. first parties which receive smaller bonuses of seats ($P_p - P_e$)

    f. first two-party pairs which receive smaller shares of the vote and seats (W_e and W_p)

    g. first two-party pairs which receive smaller bonuses of seats ($W_p - W_e$)

That these propositions are generally correct can be established by an examination of Table 7.2 below. A number of minor anomalies appear in these data, and I will discuss them below. But it is most important here that the overall correctness of the propositions contained in Differential Proposition Thirteen be established by inspection of the data themselves.

For all but two of the nine variables shown in Table 7.2, the progression of mean values for magnitude groupings is entirely consistent with the corresponding proposition. The two anomaly-producing variables are the seat bonus of the first party (row "e"), and the seat bonus of the first two parties (row "g"). The first produces one unpredicted mean value ($M = 10$–20), and the second produces two such values ($M = 2$–6 and 10–20). Even in these cases, the differences between extreme magnitude groupings is consistent with the predicted relationship. With the exceptions noted, then, it is correct to confirm Differential Proposition Thirteen. One must, of course, understand the approximate character of this analysis in evaluating the hypothesis.

TABLE 7.2
MEAN VALUES FOR PARTY SYSTEM VARIABLES
GROUPED BY DISTRICT MAGNITUDE

Party System Variable		District Magnitude Grouping			
	M = 1	M = 2–6	M = 6–10	M = 10–20	M = 120–150
a. Minimal majority (A)	1.15	1.85	1.90	2.00	2.10
b. Number of elective parties (N_e)	6.00	6.50	6.71	8.64	10.5
c. Number of legislative parties (N_p)	3.55	5.05	5.78	7.78	9.20
d. First party share of votes (P_e)	47.41%	42.21%	40.71%	33.89%	33.24%
d. First party share of seats (P_p)	55.53%	44.22%	42.66%	36.39%	34.56%
e. First party seat bonus (P_p–P_e)	8.12%	2.01%	1.95%	2.50%	1.32%
f. First two parties share of vote (W_e)	88.52%	73.73%	64.29%	59.74%	56.25%
f. First two parties share of seats (W_p)	93.98%	79.40%	67.55%	63.17%	58.44%
g. First two parties bonus of seats (W_p–W_e)	5.46%	5.67%	3.26%	3.43%	2.19%
N =	39	20	32	14	10

All of the foregoing suggests that district magnitude is an important variable. It certainly affects the proportionality or disproportionality of the seat allocations produced by electoral formulae. And it is clearly associated with a number of party system variables, although it cannot be said to "cause" the variations observed in these variables. In general, high district magnitudes are associated with multi-partism: many parties, competing on rather equal (fractionalized) terms, with the first party holding a relatively small proportion of the popular vote and legislative seats. Low district magnitudes, in contrast, appear to be associated with the properties of two-party and near-two-party systems: fewer parties, with the first two of them obtaining most of the votes and seats.

I would suggest that too much attention is generally given to the effects of electoral formulae, while too little is given to the effects of district magnitudes. The data reported here show quite clearly that the proportionality of electoral formulae depends heavily upon the number of seats assigned to each district. Since so many of the other properties of electoral systems are related to proportionality, district magnitudes must be counted along with electoral formulae among the most important aspects of electoral laws.

Complex Districting and Proportionality

In theory, one would expect complex districting—the use of two tiers of districts—to increase proportionality at any given level of magnitude.[5] The errors made at the lower level would, presumably, be canceled by opposite disproportions made at the second level. However, the four systems based on complex districting—Icelandic, German, Austrian, and Danish—do not behave in accordance with this expectation. For two of them, the German and the Danish, disproportions are below average for their respective levels of district magnitude. But for the Austrian and Icelandic systems, complex districting associates itself with greater than average disproportions, given their levels of district magnitude. Since no plausible explanation is available for the latter cases, it must be concluded that complex districting does not produce greater proportionality than simple districting at any given level of district magnitude.

* * *

The proportionality of seat allocations is related to district magnitude: the distribution of many seats in each dis-

5. For complex districting, magnitude is computed on the basis of total districts (counting both layers together).

trict is associated with relatively proportional allocations. These high-magnitude districting systems are also associated with more fractionalized party systems and with the specific properties which accompany such systems: higher minimum majorities, larger numbers of elective and legislative parties, weaker and less advantaged first parties, and weaker first two-party pairs. The present analysis allows only speculative explanation of these relationships, and no causal theory is advanced here.

The following chapter is concerned with the consequences of ordinal ballot structure.

CHAPTER 8

BALLOT STRUCTURE
AND PARTY COMPETITION

A Negative Finding

Chapter 2 suggested that ballots be divided into two general classes: (1) ordinal ballots, which allow the voter to favor more than one party with his mandate; and (2) categorical ballots, which require that the voter give his mandate to a single party. I suggested that the difference between these two classes of ballots might have the following implications for party competition:

    1. Ordinal ballots would allow each voter's mandate to be dispersed among several parties, thereby producing a sort of micro-fractionalization. Categorical ballots would prevent such an effect.

    2. Elections held with ordinal ballots would, if this micro-fractionalization were repeated over and over, produce more fractionalized elective party systems than would be found under other elections.

If this speculation were correct one would expect to find that elective party systems elected under ordinal balloting would have: (1) high fractionalization values (F_e), (2) large numbers of elective parties (N_e), (3) first parties with small shares of the total vote (P_e), and (4) first two-party pairs with small vote shares (W_e). I have tested these findings against the data and the results appear in Table 8.1.

The reader will find that my theory is absolutely wrong. In every case the comparison of the mean values contradicts my expectation. Categorical, not ordinal, balloting is associated with greater fractionalization, larger numbers of elective parties, weaker first parties, and weaker first two-party pairs. The facts of electoral politics have been cruel to my speculation on the effects of ballot structure, and I must wonder why.

TABLE 8.1
MEAN VALUES FOR FOUR ELECTIVE PARTY
SYSTEM VARIABLES: ORDINAL AND
CATEGORICAL BALLOT SYSTEMS
COMPARED

Variables	Ordinal Ballot Systems $N = 16$	Categorical Ballot Systems $N = 98$
Elective fractionalization (F_e)	0.66	0.69
Numbers of elective parties (N_e)	5.4 parties	7.25 parties
Vote share of the first party (P_e)	44.6%	41.5%
Vote share of the first two parties (W_e)	80.4%	72.1%

One methodological explanation presents itself immediately: the number of ordinal ballot elections, sixteen, is very small. It is therefore necessary to assume that the resulting mean values are less reliable than those for the larger sets analyzed elsewhere in the study. But even so, it is of interest to speculate about the actual sources of these anomalous findings. Three lines of substantive explanation suggest themselves.

First, the opportunity to divide one's mandate under

ordinal balloting procedures may be ignored by the voter. He may quite often give his vote to only one party—an act often described as "casual voting." There is some evidence that this is common practice in one ordinal system, the Australian.[1] This suggestion is consistent with the hypothesis that party identification[2]—a psychic commitment to a single party—is a deterrent to ordinal voting. For the countries involved—Luxembourg, Switzerland (one election only), Ireland, and Australia—no evidence is available on the strength or distribution of party identification, although it is clearly an important pattern in the United States. But if the electorates of these countries behave like their American counterpart, one would expect that the rather complex cognitive arrangements necessary for ordinal voting are likely to be quite rare.[3] These speculations would no doubt be worthwhile topics of research, but it is presently impossible to attribute empirical validity to them.

A second line of explanation, coordinate with the above, runs to the effect that indigenous factors in these four nations militate against party system fractionalization. Perhaps these four nations are relatively homogeneous, high consensus societies, in which the divisive forces on which opposition parties thrive are quite weak. The religious homogeneity of Eire would seem to comport with this theory. The racial homogeneity of Australian society—but not its strong class rivalries—would also seem consistent with it. The very smallness, in population and geography, of Luxembourg might also lend credibility to this thesis. And putting aside linguistic differences, it might also be argued that Switzerland is a rather homogeneous society. Perhaps, indeed, the intellectual luxury of ordinal balloting, with its apparent potential for fractionalization, can be afforded

    1. Rydon, "Election Methods," pp. 68–83.
    2. Angus Campbell et al., *The American Voter* (New York, John Wiley and Sons, 1960), pp. 120–45.
    3. Ibid., pp. 227–65.

only by rather low pressure political systems in which its effects are likely to be counteracted by other factors.

A third, and unavoidable, speculation is that ballot structure constitutes a rather weak variable. It may be much less important than electoral formulae, district magnitudes, and, more likely still, the sociopolitical forces which underlie party competition. Its potential effect may be realizable only under a very special and apparently nonexistent series of circumstances. Unfortunately, the available data allow no definitive test of this notion, and it must be left unverified.

This very brief chapter belongs to the well known, but too often suppressed, "bureau of negative results." The facts betray the theory, and we are reminded of the infinite variability of human behavior. It must also be clear that a few plausible explanations do not constitute an alternate theory.

PART III
CONCLUSIONS

CHAPTER 9

ELECTORAL LAW AS A POLITICAL INSTRUMENT

What are the political consequences of electoral laws? How do these laws affect the interests of political parties and shape the development of party systems?

In the foregoing chapters I have presented a number of answers to these questions. They are summarized at the end of each chapter and are catalogued together in Appendix A below. The task that remains is to draw these tested propositions together as the basis for some general comments on the politics of electoral law. This chapter is meant to perform that task.

Throughout the analysis I have focused attention alternately on the short run (proximal) and long run (distal) consequences of electoral laws for party competition. In this concluding chapter it will be useful to sort out these two strands of analysis, generalizing about each. The proximal effects operate at the conclusion of any single election when the legislative seats are allocated among the competing parties. The distal effects occur over the course of several elections, and follow from the proximal effects.

Proximal effects may be analyzed with great confidence since no intervening variable, save corruption, can disturb the relationship between vote and seat distributions in a given election: the electoral system is the sole connection between the two.[1] When distal effects are considered, however, the redistributive bias of electoral systems becomes only one of an infinite array of competing factors—social, psychological, economic, even accidental—and it is not easy to decide how important the effects of the electoral law itself have been in producing the observed patterns of party competition. Let us consider the two kinds of effects separately, following the natural progression from proximal to distal, factual knowledge to speculative knowledge.

Proximal Consequences of Electoral Law

For whosoever hath, to him shall be given, and he shall have more abundance: but whosoever hath not, from him shall be taken away even that he hath.
                                                                Matthew 13:12

Constants of Direction

The proximal effects of electoral laws upon political parties comport with the most literal understanding of Christ's prophecy. If a single pattern emerges from this study with status approaching a "law," it is the persistent bias of electoral laws in favor of strong parties as against their weaker competitors. The party which has many votes receives seats in "more abundance," but the party which does not have many votes is apt to receive fewer seats than its proportionate share or, worse yet, no seats at all. The prejudice of electoral laws—and here I include even the P.R. systems— in favor of strong elective parties and against weak ones is a very nearly universal fact of electoral life. This bias is reflected in three major findings:

1. Some complex proximal relationships, such as the one between district magnitude and proportionality cannot, however, be explained fully without district-by-district data.

1. Strong parties, typically those polling more than 20 per cent of the popular vote, usually receive more than proportionate shares of legislative seats; but weak parties—those polling less than 20 per cent—generally receive less than proportionate shares of the legislative seats.[2]

2. The strongest single elective party almost always receives more than its proportionate share of the seats.[3]

3. The weakest elective parties, even after trivial candidacies are discounted, are usually denied any representation whatever.[4]

As a result of these redistributions of competitive advantage, the structure of legislative politics is simplified. Parties are fewer in number; they are also, on the average, stronger. Small parties are often left out of the legislative arena, and the parties that are strong enough to obtain admittance are each likely to be stronger than they would be if electoral systems were neutral (i.e. perfectly proportional). In the categories of my analysis, these consequences can be summed up by saying that legislative party systems are less fractionalized than their elective counterparts, because electoral laws—*all* electoral laws—exert a defractionalizing effect.[5] The bias in favor of fewer, stronger parties is synonymous with the process of defractionalization.

Perhaps the most startling consequence of the defractionalizing process is the institutional creation of single-party legislative majorities.[6] When the voters fail to designate a governing majority, the electoral system may intercede to produce one by awarding a critical number of seats to the strongest of the minority parties. Indeed, almost two thirds

2. Similarity Proposition One.
3. Similarity Proposition Two.
4. Similarity Proposition Four.
5. Similarity Proposition Five.
6. Similarity Proposition Three.

of the legislative one-party majorities in the period studied were produced by this means.

These findings are not altogether inconsistent with the common-sense rule of social life: the rich get richer and the poor get poorer, most of the time. This tendency, which has been labeled "the multiplicative principle," is, according to Kaare Svalastoga, supported by a considerable evidential base.[7] It is also buttressed by common aphorisms like "money makes money," or "nothing succeeds like success." And if we remember that electoral laws are written by the leaders of parties strong enough to govern, the big party bias of actual electoral laws is not at odds with a certain disillusioned view of human nature.

There is strength in numbers. "Conformist" voters who support the leading parties are apt to be better represented (in a formal sense) than their countrymen who vote for the smaller parties. By proportionalist logic—John Stuart Mill's is the most lucid argument of the kind [8]—this is disturbing indeed. Legislatures are not clear mirrors of society; worse yet, they are always inclined to magnify the size of the "conformist" majority (or plurality) in the electorate, and to obscure many minorities. The question that is typically asked by the proportionalists is whether a given electoral law distorts representation in favor of the majority. My findings make it clear that the relevant question is not *whether* this distortion occurs, but *how great* is it?

Seen in a different light, the defractionalizing process is less disturbing. For the pragmatist, a more relevant question may be, "how can one make representative democracy work in a heterogeneous society?" How can one produce an effective flow of public policy without abandoning the elective principle in the face of many social cleavages which produce an equal number of political cleavages? How can

7. Kaare Svalastoga, *Social Differentiation* (New York, David McKay, 1965), pp. 83–104.
8. Mill, *Representative Government*, pp. 102–26.

one avoid legislative deadlocks of the kind which paralyzed the Fourth French Republic? How, within the institutional setting of liberal democracy, can one limit the divisive forces within the political system? If these are salient concerns, then the effect of electoral systems may be seen in a positive light. The defractionalizing process functions at once to: (a) improve the bargaining positions of governing parties, and (b) weaken the bargaining positions of nongoverning parties. The extremes are the manufactured majority party and the weak party denied representation.

This speculation entails a number of assumptions which might be examined specifically in each country to which the argument is applied. First, it assumes that very strong "centrifugal" forces exist and threaten to obstruct the governing process. Second, it assumes that the leaders of strong parties wish to sustain the governmental process—an assumption that is inapplicable to, say, the large French and Italian Communist parties. Third, it implies that legislative institutions already enjoy a certain legitimacy. In short, this conjecture raises more questions than it answers.

Whatever becomes of these speculations, the actual pattern remains: electoral laws work to the advantage of strong parties and to the disadvantage of weak ones. Legislative party systems are therefore defractionalized, and in many cases legislative majorities are manufactured by electoral laws. As earlier analyses demonstrated, this pattern, in which strength is added to strong parties and taken away from weak ones, is a nearly universal consequence of existing electoral laws.

Since virtually all the disproportions are credited to strong parties instead of weak ones, the redistributive effects of electoral laws proceed in only one direction. No electoral laws systematically penalize strong parties to the benefit of weak ones. The main difference between electoral laws lies, therefore, on a single continuum between perfect proportionality (where no redistribution occurs), and extreme disproportionality (where strong parties benefit most and weak ones suffer most). While the extreme of perfect proportionality is never reached in actual practice, electoral laws differ in the degree to which they diverge from it toward the extremes of strong party advantage.

Variations of Degree

The degree to which seat allocations diverge from the condition of perfect proportionality is a function of two electoral law variables: (1) electoral formulae, and (2) district magnitudes. As a rule, P.R. formulae and high district magnitudes produce more nearly proportional results, while "first-past-the-post" formulae and low district magnitudes produce the greatest disproportionality (i.e. the greatest advantage for large parties over small ones). Let me consider the two electoral law variables individually, beginning with the electoral formulae.

Electoral formulae diverge from proportionality along two institutional dimensions. First, proportional representation formulae produce smaller deviations from proportionality than "first-past-the-post" formulae, whether the latter are based on pluralities or majorities.[9] Second, highest averages P.R. formulae diverge farther from proportionality than largest remainder P.R. formulae.[10] The first difference —between P.R. and "first-past-the-post" formulae—is by far the greater of the two.

It follows that P.R. formulae are likely to minimize (but not to eradicate) the general bias of electoral formulae in favor of strong parties. P.R. formulae give a smaller advantage to the strong elective parties and exact a smaller price from weak ones.[11] They give a smaller bonus to the

9. Differential Proposition Four.
10. Differential Proposition Nine.
11. Differential Proposition One.

strongest single elective party.[12] And, naturally enough, they are less apt to deny representation to elective parties.[13]

The proportionality of seat allocation also varies with the number of seats assigned to electoral districts—district magnitudes. Where many seats are allocated in each electoral district, the outcome is likely to approximate proportionality.[14] But where fewer seats are allocated in each district, outcomes are likely to diverge more sharply from proportionality.[15] This relationship is, however, curvilinear: as district magnitudes increase, disproportionality decreases at a decreasing rate.[16] Another way to put the same thing is: as district magnitude increases, the proportionality of outcome increases at a decreasing rate.[17] One need not be surprised that the bonus obtained by the strongest party declines as district magnitude rises.[18]

Since plurality formulae are always associated with a single-member district, it is hard to distinguish the disproportionality of these formulae from that of the single-member district's low magnitude. Indeed the distinction has no empirical meaning, except in the Australian case, where a majority formula is associated with a single-member district.

Given that the defractionalization pattern, which works in favor of fewer, stronger legislative parties, is a general fact of electoral life, it is also evident that specific institutions produce variations of degree within the pattern. Political ingenuity can render the defractionalizing pattern stronger or weaker through the manipulation of the institutional variables: electoral formulae and district magnitudes.

Suppose one wanted to design an electoral law that would

12. Differential Proposition Two.
13. Differential Proposition Five.
14. Differential Proposition Ten.
15. Differential Proposition Ten.
16. Differential Proposition Eleven.
17. Differential Proposition Eleven.
18. Differential Proposition Thirteen.

maximize the defractionalizing pattern, producing strong advantages for strong parties, strong penalties for weak ones, and often "manufacturing" legislative majorities. The findings of this study suggest that the *single-member district* is the only necessary instrument. With these very low district magnitudes, the advantage of strong parties will be maximized, no matter what formula is used. Plurality and majority formulae will behave in the same way, defractionalizing legislative party systems by favoring fewer stronger parties. For that matter, even P.R. formulae would have the same effect in single-member districts. Because only one party can win in each district, the strong parties benefit at the expense of the weak ones, and legislative party systems are composed of fewer, stronger parties.[19]

Suppose, on the other hand, that one were worried about proportionality, and wished therefore to minimize defractionalization, giving each party its electoral due—no more and no less. Given these objectives, he should insist on a *P.R. formula*, preferably based on the *largest remainder procedure*, linked with *high district magnitudes* (i.e. many seats per district). It would probably not be worthwhile to expand the districts beyond ten or twenty seats, since the added proportionality seems to decline rapidly beyond that level. But with very low district magnitudes (i.e. less than six seats per district), even the largest remainder P.R. formula would produce a very substantial defractionalizing effect.

Distal Consequences of Electoral Laws

Do the short-run effects we have been discussing have long-run consequences for party systems? What are they? These questions can be answered only with considerable

19. This assertion must be modified where parties which are weak on a national scale enjoy pockets of local support, enabling them to profit from the single-member district in those areas.

caution, since party systems are influenced by many variables—social, economic, legal, and political. Proximal effect
of electoral law upon the legislative representation of parties
is to be counted only one of many determining forces. And
it is, secondly, impossible to sort out all the contributing factors, or to assign even approximate weights to them. Worse
yet, electoral laws are themselves shaped by party systems.

In the face of these difficulties, one can only suggest
limited connections. I have chosen to formulate my com-
mentary in response to the question: "Where electoral laws
do in fact make a long-run difference, which specific properties of electoral laws are apt to produce what differences?"
By choosing to work within the assumption that electoral
laws do exert long-run effects, yet without demonstrating
this assumption's validity, I have settled for a very limited
level of analysis. But to do more would require not one, but
twenty or more, developmental studies, each devoted to a
single country. The limited suggestions offered here may
provide some guidelines for research of that kind, and may
have at least tentative significance in their own right.

Party systems vary over a continuum, from non-fractionalization in one-party systems to extreme fractionalization in systems where a great many parties compete on about
equal terms. Among the party systems analyzed in this
study, the actual range of variation lies between two less
distant points: U.S.-style, two-party competition and Is-
raeli-type multi-partism. Every party system, at any one
point in time, may be assigned a place on this continuum,
although (and this is important) individual systems may
move along these scales, toward or away from the empirical
extreme of two-party competition.

How do electoral systems influence the movement of
systems on the fractionalization continuum? I wish to suggest that the pattern of proximal defractionalization described above is the source of whatever influence electoral
laws have on the fractionalization of party systems. Where

the pattern is strong—large parties are greatly advantaged
—the electoral system exerts pressure on the system for
two-party competition. But where the pattern is weak—
large parties are only slightly advantaged—a weaker, often
negligible, pressure is exerted in that direction. The defractionalizing pattern is a restraint on the fractionalization of
party systems, and the effective pressure exerted by electoral
laws varies with the intensity of the defractionalizing pattern itself. Multi-partism is most likely where electoral laws
produce a weak defractionalizing pattern, and two-party
competition most likely where the electoral laws produce a
strong defractionalizing effect.

Now, according to my earlier comments, the defractionalizing pattern is complex. It entails at least five related
subpatterns: (1) the advantage of large parties over small
ones in the division of legislative seats; (2) the awarding of
a "bonus" in seats to the strongest party; (3) the exclusion
of small parties from the legislative arena; (4) the overall
defractionalization of legislative party systems; and (5) the
fairly frequent creation of "manufactured majorities" in
legislative party systems. These are the subpatterns present
in all electoral systems, but stronger in some than others,
which constitute the defractionalizing process that seems so
important. The question thus becomes, "What electoral law
variables produce this syndrome?"

The answer to this question was foretold in the examination of proximal effects. Here let me recapitulate the effects
of these institutions, with attention to the contribution they
make to the shaping of party systems over time. Logically,
the sequence of inferences is: (a) electoral law variables to
intensity of the defractionalizing pattern, and, with less
confidence, (b) the intensity of the defractionalizing pattern to the long-run fractionalization of the party system.[20]

20. A third inference is from the degree to which an electoral system is
presently fractionalized to the kind of electoral laws adopted for future
elections.

What electoral law provisions intensify the defractional-izing pattern and therefore seem likely to exert pressure toward two-party competition? The answer is simple: the single-member district, or, failing that, small multimember districts. In a single-member district, almost any formula[21] —the plurality is most common—is likely to advantage the strong parties and, in general, to establish the defractionalizing pattern. This much is confirmed by the analysis of proximal effects. But what about the long-range effects? The findings of the study show a fairly consistent association between single-member plurality formulae and two-party systems.[22]

A causal interpretation of this association falls upon several exceptions, the clearest of which are Canadian and Austrian. Nevertheless, the combination of the proximal defracationalizing pattern and the distal association with two-party competition suggests that the single-member district is likely to contribute to the development and sustenance of two-party systems. Other factors, such as regional minorities, may reverse this condition, as is the case in Canada. But, insofar as the electoral law exerts a controlling pressure, the single-member district is likely to press the system toward two-party competition.

And what arrangements are most likely to press party systems toward multi-partism, because they exert a very weak defractionalizing effect? These would be the institutions that optimize the proportionality of outcomes: largest remainder P.R. formulae, operating in high magnitude electoral districts. Because the outcomes are more nearly proportional under these provisions, the defractionalizing process is weakened. Is there an association between these arrangements and multi-partism? The study's findings show that there is:

21. The French double ballot may be an exception, although limited evidence suggests that it is not.
22. Differential Proposition Three and Similarity Proposition Seven.

1. In general, P.R. formulae are associated with more fractionalized elective and parliamentary party systems.[23]

2. Among P.R. formula electoral laws, those using the largest-remainder procedure are associated with greater fractionalization, both elective and parliamentary, than are those using highest-average procedures.[24]

3. High district magnitudes are associated with greater fractionalization in both elective and parliamentary systems.[25]

The distal association between these institutions and high fractionalization, even when seen beside the weakness of the proximal defractionalizing pattern which they produce, does not suggest a simple *causal* relationship. It does, however, imply that insofar as the electoral law exerts a controlling pressure, these provisions are apt to press systems toward multi-partism and away from two-party competition.

These conclusions suggest that the statesman who must choose between electoral laws confronts a dilemma. On the one hand, he may opt for highly proportional election outcomes, in which case he is likely to encourage the fractionalization of party systems over time. Or, on the other hand, he may opt to encourage the development and maintenance of two parties, or less fractionalized multi-party competition, with the price being less proportional outcomes. These alternatives may not be inevitable, but the findings reported here make them seem probable: if proportionality, then multi-partism; but if two-party competition, then also a disproportional outcome.[26]

23. Differential Proposition Six.
24. Differential Proposition Nine.
25. Differential Proposition Twelve.
26. The time-sequence data for the twenty-year period I have studied do not produce clinching evidence for these speculations: except for West Germany, there is no system which changes drastically in its degree of fractionalization. But that is not altogether surprising, since all of the

Summing Up and Looking Forward

The general conclusions offered here are consistent with the specific findings of the study, yet a reasonable man might well have chosen to emphasize a different pattern. And I might well agree with *his* conclusions. Still another reader might well accept the study's findings, yet simultaneously find the general conclusions uninteresting or even, perhaps, misleading. Political discourse is marvelously subjective, especially when it touches upon issues with long polemical histories, and when it sweeps across national boundaries within which general agreement may have been reached.[27] Does this mean that the findings of this study —some of them known to the earlier literature—have added nothing useful to our knowledge about the politics of electoral law?

I hope, at least, that I have provided a number of touchstones with the facts of electoral politics. I am certainly prepared to suggest that the twenty propositions verified in this study are general and fairly accurate statements about the effects of electoral laws upon party competition. If so, it may be hoped that future arguments about the politics of electoral law will be more closely in touch with empirical reality and will, therefore, be more useful to political men who must choose between electoral laws.

But at least three series of related questions are implied, and left unanswered by the findings of the present study. First, what can a developmental analysis of elections in individual nations add to our understanding of the relation-

systems, save Germany and Israel, had been in operation for many decades before the period covered by this study. Historical analyses of the individual systems would be of interest. I must conclude that association, but not sequential data, support my speculations.

27. For example, I would hazard the guess that informed Americans, and especially American political scientists, generally agree on the appropriateness of the single-member electoral law used in America.

ship between party system and electoral law? Despite its twenty-year span, the present study is concerned largely with correlational, not chronological problems. Is it not likely that a fairly general pattern of development—resting on a large set of variables, only one of which is electoral law—underlies the contemporary party systems we have been discussing? I am intrigued by the question.

Second, what are the consequences of electoral laws for the behavior of individual politicians, operating within the confines of actual districts and party systems and moved by an infinite array of goals? How does the law shape their decision-making? And how, in turn, do these politicians act to shape the development of party systems? Further, how do the party systems so shaped come to influence the fate of electoral laws?

Third, how do party systems influence politics in general? What is the consequence of fractionalization for government stability and for the capacity of legislative politics to resolve the issues of the day? [28] How might defractionalization—the common bias of electoral systems in favor of a few strong parties—influence the fate of minorities as they compete with majorities? What are the consequences of electoral law and party system for the viability of the government–opposition tension which is so important to our cherished notion of liberal democracy?

These questions suggest three distinct directions for future research: (1) back in time toward the analysis of development; (2) inward toward the behavioral complexities of individual systems; and (3) outward toward the consequences of electoral politics for politics in general.

I have tried to isolate a series of general relationships between party system and electoral law for one period in the history of liberal democracy. These relationships have an in-

28. Since our measure of fractionalization is based on the probability of partisan disagreement, the data reported in this study may have a direct relevance for this very interesting question.

terest of their own, and may add something to the century-old literature on the politics of electoral law. Hopefully, they will also facilitate the work of the scholar whose interests have carried him in one of the directions mentioned here or in yet another, unexplored direction.

CHAPTER 10

PROPORTIONAL REPRESENTATION, THE MULTIPLICATION OF PARTIES, AND GOVERNMENT INSTABILITY

The association between proportional representation and multiparty systems has provoked a great deal of largely undisciplined speculation since the Europeans began adopting P.R. schemes three generations ago. The nub of the argument is that P.R. allows more and more insurgent parties to gain access to parliaments, fractionalizing parliamentary party systems and leading to the eventual destabilization of parliamentary governments. One author carries this analysis as far as to associate the rise of Hilter's National Socialism with the P.R. electoral formula used during the Weimar regime, eventually crushed by that movement,[1] and another suggests that P.R.'s effect is so strong that its adoption weakens government to the point of inviting military conquest (presumably on the part of strong, P.R.-free neighbors!).[2] The correlational analysis reported in the preceding chapters of this book is not designed to test the explanatory merits of this argument, though it does cast some doubt on the universality of its application (see chapters 4 and 5 above). Here, I would like to report some analytic results

1. F. A. Hermans, *Democracy or Anarchy?* (South Bend, Ind.: Notre Dame University Press, 1941).
2. Duncan Black, *The Theory of Committees and Elections* (Cambridge: Cambridge University Press, 1958), pp. 82–83.

bearing more directly on the alleged P.R. syndrome. To begin at the end, the major results are these:

1. P.R. is neither a necessary nor a sufficient condition for the insurgence of new parliamentary parties.

2. The ease with which insurgent parties may gain access to parliaments is a joint function of seven structural variables, only one of which is the electoral formula (P.R. v. plurality).

3. Compared with a plurality system, P.R. *raises* the minimum share of the national vote required to win representation for an insurgent.

4. Neither under P.R. formulae nor under plurality formulae is it possible for a party to win representation with a share of the national vote lower than one over n,[3] the number of parties, times r, the number of seats in the legislature $(1/(n \cdot r))$.

5. In comparison to plurality formulae, P.R. *lowers* the maximum share of the national vote that can fail to win representation for an insurgent party.

6. Geographic distributions of votes for the insurgent party and its rivals are critically important in determining whether or not it gains access to representation.

And, finally, on the question of government instability,

7. The number of parliamentary parties is positively related to government instability, but the fractionalization of parliamentary party systems is more strongly related to instability, and the best structural "explanation" for government instability is the joint effect of anti-system parties and the fractionalization of pro-system parties in parliament.[4]

3. In the remainder of this section, we will use n to represent the number of elective parties, without the subscript e. An exception occurs below on p. 171.

4. This result rests on an exploratory correlational analysis carried out by Michael Taylor and Valantine Herman, "Party Systems and Government Stability," *American Political Science Review,* 65 (1971), 28–37.

The joint effect of these seven propositions is to undermine whatever straightforward simplicity the "P.R.-multiplication-instability" syndrome might otherwise possess. What emerges is a sense of complex interdependence, with electoral formulae playing only one part in the overall pattern. Let me begin with a word on method.

In dealing with problems of this kind, correlational analysis is not always useful, even when it is based on "before and after" comparisons of the kind proposed by Duverger.[5] This is because history offers no controlled experiments, and empirical correlations are necessarily subject to spuriousness—in this case, to the possibility that the multiplication of parties *and* the adoption of P.R. arise from common underlying forces. If it were possible to draw up an exhaustive list of these underlying forces, if the list were of finite length, and if we could find examples where all these forces did and did not occur, it would be possible to design a controlled analysis. But, since the innumerable candidates for the role of "underlying force"—economic conditions, social histories, political events—are ill defined and subject to almost infinite revision, this strategy is unavailable to us.[6] If we are to deal with the issue—as the correlational analysis reported in the earlier chapters of this book cannot—an analytic strategy seems essential.

By "analytic strategy" I mean an argument that generates logical relations having an "if-then," conditional structure. Without trying to predict the "ifs"—the social circumstances leading to the formation of a new electoral party for example—one tries to generate statements about what will happen in light of other variables—such as the existence of a given electoral formula—should the "ifs" materialize. This produces partial explanatory knowledge with a standing in-

5. *Political Parties*, trans. Barbara and Robert North (New York: John Wiley and Sons, 1954).

6. The expansibility of this list accounts for what Aaron Wildavsky calls the "and-so fallacy" in "A Methodological Critique of Duverger's *Political Parties*," *Journal of Politics*, 21 (1959), 303–18.

dependent of the unexplained factors leading to the initial emergence of new parties. All but the last of the seven propositions considered here rest on an analysis of this variety.

The most serious attempt at an analysis of this kind is Colin Leys's "Models, Theories, and the Theory of Political Parties,"[7] in which he attempts to explain the number of parties found in any given political system by means of a formal model. The effort is suggestive but suffers from two rather important shortcomings. The first is its reliance on an over-deterministic and rather implausible assumption: the number of "bodies of opinion" at any point in time is a (positively) lagged function of the number of parties at an earlier time. This generalization substitutes a quite arbitrary, often incorrect claim for a genuinely uncertain relationship.[8] The present analysis avoids this particular form of brittleness. Second, Leys's model leads to no concrete predictions but rather to an abstract suggestion of equilibrium. This in itself is quite all right, but if we are interested in the role of specific structures, it is not helpful. Leys does insert an idealized P.R. formula, without considering any of the complexities entailed by actual systems. The present analysis tries to say less but to say it more concretely on the basis of a less brittle superstructure. Let me begin with the connection between P.R. and the multiplication of parties and finish with the related problem of government instability.

P.R. and the Multiplication of Parties

The simplest and most attractive analyses of the connection between P.R. and the multiplication of parties are unavailable to us:

1. *P.R. is neither a necessary nor a sufficient condition for the insurgence of new parliamentary parties.*

7. Harry Eckstein and David Apter, eds., *Comparative Politics* (New York: The Free Press, 1963), pp. 305–15.
8. By "uncertain" I mean that no generally predictable pattern should be expected, and *if* any such pattern is obtained, I would be inclined to think it negative rather than positive.

By *insurgence*, we do not, of course, mean the initial establishment of a system's strongest parties—for example, the Third Republic French Radicals or the American Jeffersonian Democrats or the Israeli Mapai. Nor do we mean the futile efforts of parties that fail to gain access to parliaments —for example, the dozen-odd fringe parties offering politically meaningless candidates in most elections. By insurgence we mean that a party for the first time wins one or more parliamentary seats despite the opposition of two or more established parties. Obvious examples would include British Labour at the turn of the century, the Canadian Social-Credit Party of recent decades, a host of European Socialist and Communist and Christian Democratic parties—all cases in which a new party gained entry to parliament over established opposition.

It requires no rigorous analysis to show that P.R. is neither necessary nor sufficient for insurgencies of this kind. First, P.R. is hardly necessary for the insurgency of a very powerful new party—British Labour, for example—and cannot be considered a precondition to the genesis of such parties: factors well beyond electoral arrangements are involved in that. Second, even when an insurgent arises to contest an election, P.R. is not enough in itself to guarantee its representation.[9] But, most conclusively, it is possible to imagine circumstances in which an insurgent would win representation under a plurality system and not under a P.R. system. Suppose, in some geographic segment of an electorate, that an insurgent party appears with a nodule of support amounting to 5 per cent of the sector's voting population and that this nodule lies in a subarea compact enough that its total vote is about 10 per cent of the area total. Under a plurality formula, it would be possible to divide the sector into ten single-member districts—one surrounding the insurgent party's

9. For example, the empirical evidence in the original study indicated that an average of 0.79 nontrivial parties were excluded by P. R. formulae. See p. 97 above.

support—and for the new party to win that seat. Now consider a P.R. system applied to the same area. Perhaps ten seats will be allocated in a single district covering the whole sector. The insurgents will amount now to only 5 per cent of the district total, and (under any P.R. formula) it may be excluded from representation (save the improbable case in which 19 or more competitors divide their votes equally). However contrived the example, its implications are strong enough to rule out any solution resting on logical necessity.

This example goes well beyond the implications of our first proposition, suggesting that a P.R. formula is neither a necessary nor a sufficient condition for the insurgence of new parties—indeed may even point in the opposite direction—*without* recourse to the vagaries of underlying factors responsible for the initial emergence of new electoral parties. Indeed, electoral formulae are imbedded in a complex net of structural variables and depend for their implications on the values taken by six other variables.

> 2. *The ease with which an insurgent party may gain access to parliaments is a joint function of seven structural variables, only one of which is the electoral formula (P.R. v. plurality).*

a. Most important, of course, is the success enjoyed by the insurgent party in winning votes, its *proportion of the national vote* (T). If, to begin with an absurdity, it should win half the national vote, then no combination of our six remaining variables could result in its exclusion (and precious few would result in its winning anything less than majority control of parliament). On the other hand, an insurgent party receiving less than a certain minimum share of the vote could not enter the parliamentary arena under any circumstance (see Proposition 4, this chapter). What we will need to establish, by considering the joint effects of the six remaining variables, are some cutoff points, or thresholds, which tell us when, if at all, a given proportion of the national vote can win representation for an insurgent party. These thresholds will in turn allow us to isolate and define the impact of P.R. formulae in relation to other variables.

   b. Almost equally important is the *spatial distribution of the party's vote*. There are, of course, innumerable distributions for a vote of any given size between the districts of an electorate. In Figure 10.1, a number of possible distributions are shown for a party having some fixed proportion of the total vote. Districts on the left are the ones in which the party does best; those on the right, in which it does worst. Now, if we want to know the capacity of such a party to break through the opposition of established parties to win representation, then our interest centers on the way these distributions affect its chances of winning *some* seats, one or more, rather than its capacity to win any given number. From this point of view, the most advantageous distributions —under any electoral formula—are those that concentrate rather than disperse support. These distributions maximize the party's share of the district vote in its "best" districts, minimize the number of votes "wasted" in hopeless districts. It may happen that less concentrated distributions will be equally advantageous—as with Israeli-style P.R.—but there are no cases in which they will be more advantageous. In Figure 10.1, the two solid-line curves represent the extreme cases: the L-curve maximum concentration, the flat one minimum concentration. The broken curves represent a few of the intervening cases. These extreme cases are used to define "thresholds" below. For the lower, more "optimistic" threshold (T_1), we assume maximum concentration (the L-curve) and for the upper, more pessimistic threshold (T_2), we assume minimum concentration (the flat curve).

   We will also need to deal with intermediate cases, and two measures are used for this purpose. First, a party's *absolute concentration* is the proportion of its total national vote concentrated in its "best" district. And second, its *relative concentration* is this proportion divided by the proportion of

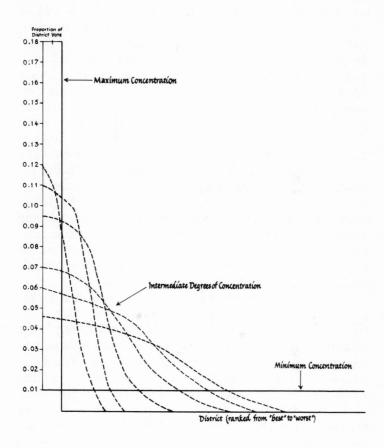

Figure 10.1

SOME POSSIBLE DISTRIBUTIONS OF AN INSURGENT PARTY'S
VOTE BETWEEN DISTRICTS

the electorate at large found within the same district.[10] Thus if a party had 0.2 of its national vote in a district comprising 0.1 of the electorate, the relative concentration would be 2.0. This may be thought of as the ratio between its maximum concentration and its mean concentration: the "best" district is, in our example, twice as densely peopled with supporters as the average district. This rather awkward measure is important because we must compare systems containing many small districts (e.g. plurality) with systems having few large ones (e.g. P.R.), and we will wish to discuss the extent to which a party's support must be so concentrated under the two systems if it is to attain representation.

c. Also relevant is the *number of parties*. Including the insurgent, we consider competition among n parties. This numerical variable is important because it affects the lower threshold—the minimum proportion of the national vote required to win representation if every other variable takes on optimal value. Roughly, the larger number of parties under any electoral system, the lower the minimum possible vote proportion which can win representation.

d. If the insurgent party is the nth contender, it is important to see how its n — 1 adversaries divide their share of the vote, and especially to see how they divide their votes in the nth party's "best" district. As may be seen from Appendix E, on district payoff functions, the insurgent party wins a seat with a lower share of the district vote where the n — 1 other parties divide their votes evenly, only with a higher share of the vote when one of the n — 1 parties gets every vote not obtained by the nth party. This variable, *the partisan distribution of votes not won by the insurgent*, also separates our two threshold functions. The upper threshold (T_2) as-

10. While absolute concentration has an upper limit of one, relative concentration has an upper limit of infinity. Its lower limit is one, where there is one district or where its support is distributed evenly over each of several districts. These indices waste a great deal of information, but the information lost is not directly relevant to the analysis: the indices and the analysis focus on points of maximum concentration.

sumes that the opposition vote is concentrated in the hands of a single strong party, at least in the insurgent's strongest district, while the lower threshold assumes that it is divided evenly amongst that party's $n - 1$ rivals. Here again, the analysis of extreme cases allows us to define ranges, and we may use these to identify the marginal impact of a P.R. formula.

e. The *electoral formula* is, of course, our central concern. For simplicity, I have let the d'Hondt highest averages formula represent the general class of Proportional Representation.[11] This is because the d'Hondt accounts for nearly two-thirds of the P.R. formulae used in the elections of Western democracies since World War II. Other formulae do behave differently, as the empirical results reported earlier in this book suggest, and I have given some contrasting values for them in footnotes later in this section. But, since the analysis is relatively complicated, I have confined the main argument to a single formula, and hereafter "P.R." should be understood in this restricted sense. The plurality formula, of course, presents no ambiguities of definition.

f. The "P.R.-ness" of a P.R. system depends, as suggested earlier (Chapter 7), on the *magnitudes of electoral districts* (m), and this variable turns out to be crucial here as well. We allow this variable to range from one (in plurality systems) to the total size of the legislature (r) as in the one-district version of P.R. (e.g. the Israeli Knesset). For simplicity, the analysis presented below assumes equally apportioned districts of equal magnitude. So, in one example, we assume a one-hundred-seat chamber divided into 2 or 4 or 5 or 20 or 25 or 50 districts of equal magnitude with equal voting populations. This is, of course, empirically inaccurate, but it serves to give a useful approximation of real systems, and adjustments to less symmetrical systems may easily (if inelegantly) be accomplished.

11. See pp. 31–33 above.

g. Finally, the *size of the legislature* to be elected exerts some influence of its own, and this generally neglected variable (we label it r) is included.

Either in defining thresholds or in plotting their analytic relations, all seven of these variables play some part. Let us now turn to an analysis of the numerical obstacles faced by an insurgent party under P.R. and plurality systems. The first result is, perhaps, unexpected.

> 3. *Compared with a plurality system, P.R. raises the minimum share of the national vote required to win representation for an insurgent.*

It is important to see that this rather unexpected result applies to one set of rather special circumstances. First, let the number of parties (n) and the size of the legislature (r) be the same for a P.R. and plurality case. Then suppose that the insurgent party enjoys maximum absolute concentration; we are, in practice, thinking about localized insurgencies. And finally, suppose that the established parties are obliging enough to divide their own votes evenly in the district where the insurgent is strongest. The district magnitudes will be one for plurality and a larger number ($1 < m \leq r$) for P.R. This is an extreme case, defining the absolute minimum share of the national vote which can—under the "perfect" configuration of the structural variables—win representation for a party. Now we wish to calculate the minimum vote share (T_1 we label it) which can, in this happy instance, win representation for an insurgent under plurality and P.R. formulae.

In order to win a first seat under a plurality formula, the insurgent needs to surpass one n^{th} of a district vote, and—assuming the fair apportionment mentioned above—this district total will be one r^{th} of the total national vote. The threshold value is therefore the product of these two fractions:

$$T_1 \text{ (plurality)} = \frac{1}{n} \cdot \frac{1}{r} = \frac{1}{nr}$$

If the legislature contained, say, two hundred seats and there were five parties including the insurgent, this would mean that one-thousandth (0.001) of the national vote could win representation under a plurality formula. This is empirically improbable, but it does help to explain the earlier finding that "Plurality formulae are associated with two-party competition *except where strong local minority parties exist*" (Differential Proposition Three above).

Under a P.R. formula, the minimum proportion of a district vote that can possibly win representation is $1/(m + n - 1)$ (see Appendix E). And, on the assumption of symmetrical districting, the district's total vote must amount to m/r^{th}s of the national total. The minimum possible vote that can win an insurgent party representation under P.R. thus becomes the product of these two fractions:

$$T_1 \text{ (P.R.)} = \frac{1}{(m + n - 1)} \cdot \frac{m}{r} = \frac{m}{r(m + n - 1)}$$

If the legislature contained two hundred seats, and there were five parties contesting ten districts of twenty seats each, the threshold would lie at $1/240^{th}$ of the national total, or 0.004. This numerical result is four times as high as the plurality analog just described, but this does not demonstrate our proposition that P.R. *always* raises this threshold. The proposition is, nevertheless, universally correct, as the following algebraic demonstration shows:

Proposition 3 $\rightarrow \dfrac{m}{r(m + n - 1)} > \dfrac{1}{n \cdot r}$ \hfill (1)

And, by the definition of the problem, \hfill (2)

$$m > 1 \text{ (for P.R.)}$$
$$n \geq 2$$

(1) implies that

$$m \cdot n \cdot r > r(m + n - 1)$$

And, dividing by r,

$$m \cdot n > m + n - 1$$

(2) requires that both m and n exceed one, which assures that their product is larger than their sum, proving that the

initial inequality (1) must hold for all permissible values of the variables.[12] Proposition 3 is therefore always correct analytically.

We can, in other words, be sure that plurality systems set a lower absolute minimum on national vote shares than P.R. systems for small parties seeking access to parliamentary representation and that this is true for all values of the relevant variables. It happens that the proposition becomes "truer"—in the sense that the difference between thresholds grows larger—as the magnitudes of P.R. electoral districts grow larger. In Figure 10.2, the solid curve rising from the origin represents T_1 (P.R.), and the dotted line at the bottom allows one to compare its value with the plurality analog. The vertical axis is logarithmic so as to exaggerate this difference, and one must remember that the difference is never terribly great, being at most $(n-1)/(n \cdot r)$. The same analysis also permits one subsidiary result.

> 4. *Neither under P.R. formulae nor under plurality formulae is it possible for a party to win representation with a share of the national vote lower than one over n, the number of parties, times r, the number of seats in the legislature ($1/(n \cdot r)$).*

This follows immediately from the threshold value for plurality ($1/n \cdot r$) and the demonstration of Proposition 3.[13] Both Propositions 3 and 4 deal with the extreme case in which six structural variables take their most favorable values and electoral formula is allowed to vary. But it is equally impor-

---

12. This result does *not* apply to Largest Remainder formulae. It would hold only if

$$\frac{m}{r(2m+n-1)} > \frac{1}{n-r}$$

This is not true for permissible values of the variables, since it implies $mnr > 2mr + nr - r$, which is false if $n \geq 2$. The initial inequality is derived by an inference similar to that followed here for d'Hondt formulae.

13. Similarly, it follows immediately that it does *not* apply to Largest Remainder P.R. See note 12 above.

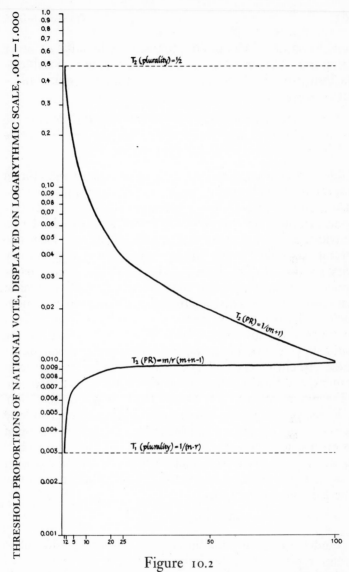

Figure 10.2

THRESHOLD CURVES FOR P.R. COMPARED WITH PLURALITY
THRESHOLD POINTS $(r — 100, n — 3, m — 1\text{-}100,$ VERTICAL
SCALE LOGARYTHMIC$)$

tant to consider the opposite extreme, in which the six other structural variables take values as unfavorable as possible to the insurgent. This "pessimistic" view leads to a quite different conclusion.

> 5. *In comparison to plurality formulae, P.R. lowers the maximum share of the national vote that can fail to win representation for an insurgent party.*

Here, we consider the least favorable circumstances for an insurgent party. Suppose—with n and r constant—that the insurgent party's vote shows minimum absolute and relative concentration, being evenly distributed across each of r/m districts. Suppose further that in each of these, it faces one strong established party (though the particular party may vary from district to district). We are thinking in practice about insurgents without local focus competing against established parties with such foci, either by reason of demography or by reason of strategic "district-trading" carried out to repress the insurgent party. The largest share of the national vote that could fail to win representation under these circumstances will fail to do so under *any* circumstances, and these circumstances define the upper threshold (T_2) above which a party cannot fail to win representation.

In the plurality case, a party could lose a district so long as its vote did not exceed half the district total, and because of its even spatial distribution, the party could have up to half of the vote in each of m such districts. It *could*, in other words, fail to win representation with a vote share up to one-half the national total:

$$T_2 \text{ (plurality)} = \frac{1}{2}$$

Under a P.R. formula, in contrast, a party could fail to attain representation so long as its vote did not exceed $1/(m + 1)$ of any district total. A party could fail to win representation up to this share of the vote in each district, and, on the assumption of even distribution, up to the same share of the national vote:

$$T_2 \text{ (P.R.)} = \frac{1}{m + 1}$$

This quantity declines rather dramatically as district magnitudes increase. In the meaningless case of m = 1, it would be one-half, but it declines rapidly, reaching the value $1/(r + 1)$ in the one-district case. This is represented by the solid curve which begins at the upper left in Figure 10.2. Its relevance lies in *guaranteeing* representation to relatively smaller and smaller insurgents as district magnitudes increase. So, in the case of one district and two hundred seats, a party with a vote share of about 0.005 would be sure of winning a seat. Another implication, perhaps more important historically, is that P.R. sets a substantially lower barrier against the representation of nationally dispersed insurgents than does plurality election.

The proof of Proposition 5 is trivial: If m is (as it must be) greater than one for P.R., then $1/(m + 1)$ must exceed one-half.[14] The proposition is then analytically correct.

Data from the original study illustrate the patterns suggested by Propositions 3 and 5. The smallest share of a national vote to win representation for a party occurred under a plurality system, when a splinter group from the Canadian Commonwealth Federation won representation in exchange for only 6,402 of 5,296,130 votes cast, a proportion of 0.00121. Since 245 members were returned, and there were nineteen parties, the lower limit with a plurality formula in that 1945 election was 0.00022, easily permitting this miniparty to win representation. And the corresponding P.R. limit was high enough not to have permitted it, provided

14. The same is true of Largest Remainder formulae, since the relevant inequality is

$$\frac{1}{2m} < \frac{1}{2}$$

which is necessarily the case provided m > 1.

ṁ were 8 or more (at m = 245, the P.R. limit is 0.0038).[15] By comparison, the smallest vote share to win representation under a P.R. formula belonged to the Sardinian Action Party, which won a seat for 64,201 of 25,828,261 votes in the Italian election of 1948, a share of 0.00249. While the representation of parties as small as these is fairly rare under any electoral system, they do help to illustrate the operation of the rather abstract relationships being considered here. To take the contrary cases, the largest vote share that failed to obtain representation occurred under a plurality, not a P.R. formula. In the general election of 1954, the New Zealand Social Credit party won over one-tenth of the national vote (0.112) without managing to win a single seat. In comparison, the largest vote share failing to win representation under a P.R. formula was that of the "non-Socialist combined list" in Norway's 1949 election, where 106,959 of 1,748,246 votes (0.0612) failed to win representation.

As Figure 10.2 and these cursory examples suggest, the effect of P.R. is to "raise the floor and lower the ceiling," as T_1 increases with m and T_2 declines, until—in the case of m = r—they meet, and the importance of spatial distributions disappears. As districts grow larger, the relationship between a party's vote and its chance for representation becomes increasingly determinate. This is a partial explanation for the findings of Chapter 7, which suggest that propor-

---

15. The turning point is m = 8 for the following reason. If the inequality is to hold, we require that:

$$\frac{m}{r(m+n-1)} \geq .00121$$

and, since n = 19 and r = 245

$$\frac{m}{245(m+18)} \geq .00121$$

$$m \geq (0.29645)\ (m+18)$$
$$.70355m > 5.33610$$
$$m \geq 7.036$$

And, since m is an integer, m = 8. The force of the Italian P.R. examples given below is diminished by its having occurred under an *Imperiali*, not a d'Hondt formula.

tionality was related to district magnitude. And it suggests a general rule of thumb for the effect of electoral systems on the insurgency of small parties: assuming very large districts, P.R. favors nationally dispersed insurgents (lowering the point at which they can *and* will win representation to the neighborhood of $1/r$), while plurality systems (and to a lesser degree, small district P.R.) favor regionally concentrated insurgents. Proposition 6 is a logical consequence of Propositions 3 and 5: insofar as the two lead to different conclusions, which they surely do, then spatial distributions are crucial.

6. *Geographic distributions of vote for the insurgent party and its rivals are of critical importance in determining whether or not it gains access to representation.*

Remembering, of course, the special case of one-district P.R. as an exception, this generalization needs no demonstration independent of the specific propositions on which it is based (3 and 5).

6.1. *It should also, as we have suggested, be clear that distributions grow more important as m/r declines and districts become more numerous.*

Finally, it may be of some interest to ask just how concentrated support for a party of given size must be to win representation. Assuming a given share of the national vote, T, we may answer this question for "best" and "worst" cases, depending on our assumption about the distribution of votes among other parties. Table 10.1 gives analytic values for the required degrees of relative and absolute concentration. Without repeating each derivation, let me illustrate with the simplest case—plurality on the "worst case" assumption. The insurgent party's total vote is T, and we want first to know the required degree of absolute concentration—the fraction of T which must be in the party's strongest district. In that district, it must have one-half of one r^{th} of the national vote ($1/2r$) in its best district. What part of T is this?

TABLE 10.1
DEGREES OF CONCENTRATION REQUIRED TO WIN REPRESENTATION FOR PARTY WITH NATIONAL VOTE SHARE T[a]

Formula	Distribution of Other Party Votes	Minimum Necessary Absolute Concentration	Minimum Necessary Relative Concentration
P.R.	best case	$\dfrac{m}{Tr(m+n-1)}$	$\dfrac{1}{T(m+n-1)}$
Plurality	best case	$\dfrac{1}{Tn \cdot r}$	$\dfrac{1}{Tn}$
P.R.	worst case	$\dfrac{m}{Tr(m+1)}$	$\dfrac{1}{T(m+1)}$
Plurality	worst case	$\dfrac{1}{2Tr}$	$\dfrac{1}{2T}$

[a]Values for relative concentration below 1.0 indicate that a party would win representation with *any* spatial distribution.

$$\text{Required Absolute Concentration} = \left(\frac{\frac{1}{2r}}{T}\right) = \frac{1}{2rT}$$

Thus, if a party had won 10 per cent of the national vote, and there were a total of one hundred seats, the required degree of absolute concentration would be

$$\frac{1}{2 \cdot 100 \cdot (0.1)} = \frac{1}{20} = .05$$

and 5 per cent of the party's national total would therefore have to be concentrated in its best district. But this may be misleading if we are to make comparisons between systems where districts contain different fractions of the national total. Here we consider relative concentration, which is the party's absolute concentration divided by the proportion of the electorate found in a given district. We have $\dfrac{1}{2rT}$ in a district amounting to $\dfrac{1}{r}^{\text{th}}$ of the electorate.

$$\text{Required Relative Concentration} = \dfrac{\dfrac{1}{2rT}}{\dfrac{1}{r}} = \dfrac{r}{2rT} = \dfrac{1}{2T}$$

Thus, if the party's total vote were 0.10 of the national total, it would need a relative concentration of:

$$\frac{1}{2 \cdot (0.1)} = \frac{1}{0.2} = 5.0$$

Its best district would thus have to contain five times the concentration of votes found in its mean district (e.g. five times 0.1 = 0.5 of the best district vote).

These requirements for concentration cut in two directions. The required level of absolute concentration is always higher for the P.R. cases, the relative concentration level is always higher for plurality. Proposition 3—that plurality admits smaller parties—reflects what happens with high absolute concentration under first-past-the-post systems, and Proposition 5—that maximum exclusion levels are lower with P.R.—is independent of concentration requirements. I will not trouble the reader with algebraic demonstrations here, but (if it is remembered that T must be less than one) the inequalities are straightforward.

The six results sketched out so far suggest a complex and rather richly interconnected pattern of structural variation. From the view they present it is clearly silly to conclude that P.R. causes the multiplication of parties. Strictly speaking, it would be at least as accurate to say that large legislatures have this effect. I suspect that the intuitive basis for naïve speculation on P.R. and the multiplication of parties rests tacitly on a comparison between P.R. and plurality *in one district*—giving the impression that P.R. always offers lower thresholds for successful insurgency. This is of course a misleading comparison that flatly misses the problem's complexity. If there is a connection between P.R. and the multiplication of parties in some national histories, it results from a complex set of contingencies similar to those outlined here, not from the operation of a general law. And in those contingencies, P.R. can—by definition and in fact—play only one of several parts.

This is not, however, an argument for casual reduction to "underlying forces." It is, of course, true that the seven structural variables we have discussed do ultimately reflect the direct and indirect consequences of other forces. One might, to pick an extreme example, say that the territorial pattern of plurality elections in English-speaking nations in part reflects the system of shire delegations adopted in fourteenth-century England to keep Edward I in touch with one source of political resistance. And it is no doubt correct to say that working-class alienation—or its determining correlates in economic organization—helps to explain the success of insurgent Left parties throughout Europe over the past eighty years. These and many other reductive arguments may be quite valid, but, taken alone, they fail to explain the pattern that interests us here. Their impact on our problem rests wholly on the ways in which they shape the contingent relationships among structural variables—including the sizes and distributions of party votes or, for that matter, the events leading to the adoption of an electoral formula. However one explains the pattern of structural variables that emerges in a given history, what must not be overlooked is the fact that everything depends on patterns of relation *between* variables, rather than the values taken by variables in isolation.

We are left, then, with a structural account for the multi-plication of parties that *does not compete with but rather mediates the surrounding envelope of societal forces*. If I am correct in thinking that the seven variables discussed here offer a potentially complete structural account, then there can be no question of other forces *intervening* to alter their combined effect on the success of insurgent parties. The role of these other forces is instead to explain the particular con-figuration of structural variables which do in fact occur at given points in time for given national histories. Their impact is felt *through* their determination of structural configura-tions, which in turn fix the conditions of partisan insurgency. Without anything like proof, I am inclined to think that no terribly general pattern of determination will be found in these underlying variables.

There is, however, one important pattern that is suggested by the major finding of the original study. In most cases, electoral systems function to the advantage of large estab-lished parties and to the disadvantage of small established parties and insurgents. Now, if the leaders of an established party (or coalition) could control the choice of an electoral formula, a system of districting, and (within limits) the size of a legislature, they would be able to manipulate many of the structural variables we have discussed. First, by drawing districts properly, it is possible to influence enormously the relative concentration of a party's support—slicing its vote into many parts or concentrating it in a single district. Sec-ond, by forming electoral alliances or "trading districts," established parties can manipulate another important vari-aule and confront an insurgent party with a single strong competitor at every turn. Third, by choosing electoral formulae and district magnitudes to complement the out-comes of these manoeuvres, operative thresholds can be manipulated to the disadvantage of the insurgent. All this cannot, of course, be done every time an insurgent appears, but it can be carried out often enough to explain a part of the "defractionalizing" prejudice exhibited by most electoral systems in practice.

Finally, it may be worth noting the one consequence that P.R. and large districts can be said to produce most directly: a tendency to reduce the advantage of small insurgents with highly localized nodules of support vis-à-vis insurgents without such concentrated support. Under a plurality system, one should expect concentrated insurgents to do much better than dispersed ones (the Canadian case for example), but under P.R. systems this should be a much less decisive advantage. It is just possible that P.R., along with the technologies of transport and communication, serves as a brake against territorial differentiation, removing as it does one major incentive. If this is so—and we are by now well into the realm of conjecture—then an ironic conclusion may result: P.R. may, in the special case of territorial minorities, serve as a check *against* minority representation. Or, more exactly, P.R. may remove the special advantage that plurality systems give to such minorities when they seek representation.

We return now to the argument with which the chapter began. Having demonstrated, conclusively I think, that no simple (or unidirectional) relationship links P.R. to the multiplication of parliamentary parties, the question of government stability remains.

Election Outcomes and Government Stability

It is generally supposed that election outcomes—allocations of seats among parties—quite directly determine which party or coalition will control a parliamentary government. So, for example, one of our most sophisticated accounts holds out these conditions for representative democracy: "A single party (or coalition of parties) is chosen by popular election to run the governing apparatus," and "Any party (or coalition of parties) receiving the support of a majority of those voting is entitled to take over the powers of government until the next election."[16] It is revealing that these requirements, most obviously the second, lead to logical contradictions and must therefore be violated by any empirical system of parliamentary politics. Since this logical difficulty carries our attention toward an important empirical question, let me begin by examining it briefly.

During a campaign, we have n_e parties. Before the electorate decides, one can imagine that any of $2^{n_e} - 1$ parties or coalitions might command majorities and form a government. Thus, with three electoral parties one can imagine $2^3 - 1 = 7$ conceivable governments (e.g. A, B, C, AB, AC, BC, ABC.) According to "common sense" and Downs's stipulations, the election outcome should reduce this set of possibilities to one, *the* party or coalition which commands a majority. But if more than one party wins representation, this cannot be literally true. If n_p parties win representation, the election outcome must leave open the possibility of exactly 2^{n_p-1} distinct majority governments. The effect of an election outcome is thus to reduce the set of potential majority governments without "picking" a single government. If, for example, three parties win representation, then exactly $2^{3-1} = 4$ possible governments must remain *no matter how seats are divided among these parties*. And this implies that both of Downs's requirements are unrealizable: the election itself cannot pick *a* party or coalition to govern, and

16. Anthony Downs, *An Economic Theory of Democracy* (New York: Harper & Row, 1957) pp. 23–24. A related but less clearcut difficulty arises in Robert Dahl's notion of polyarchy, when it is required that alternatives with more votes replace alternatives with fewer. See *A Preface to Democratic Theory* (Chicago: University of Chicago Press, 1956), Chap. 3. In both cases, the problem arises, I think, because the authors are thinking primarily about two-party systems and only secondarily about multiparty systems. In Dahl's analysis the requirement is stated as an ideal, but in Downs's it is treated (incorrectly) as a feature which "in practice" distinguishes democracy from other forms.

some parties or coalitions holding majorities must inevitably be denied control of government (e.g. $2^{np-1} = 1$). This very formal difficulty is not without its relevance to experience.

If a single party wins a majority of its own, the difficulty is merely technical. Say that A holds a majority over B and C. It is still true that the election permits four possible governments (A, AB, AC, ABC,) but there are compelling reasons to presume that one will be chosen (A). In this event, we need only add the stipulation that potential governments with inessential members (AB, AC, ABC, in our example) may be ignored. One might suppose that the problem could thus be reduced to a linguistic quibble were it not for the fact that about two-thirds of all parliamentary elections fail to produce single-party majorities (of 107 elections analyzed in the original study, only 8 produced natural majorities, 25 produced manufactured majorities, and the remaining 74 produced neither). Thus a more typical case occurs when no single party holds a majority and one is left without an obvious choice of govenment. Thus, if A, B, and C each have less than half the seats in a parliament, then the possible governments include AB, AC, BC, and ABC. This is a more than technical violation of Downs's requirement, for it leaves an open set of potential governments (and, significantly, a choice of potential alternatives to any government that forms).

A useful example is offered by the 1963 election of the Icelandic parliament (the *Althingi*). The Independence Party obtained 24 seats, the Progessives 19, the Communists 8, and the Social Democrats 7. With four electoral parties, one might have imagined $2^4 - 1 = 15$ possible governments, and (since no party was denied representation) the outcome simply restricts this to a subset of $2^{4-1} = 8$ groupings that command majorities and could conceivably form governments. To each of these, there naturally corresponds a potential set of opposition parties:

	Possible Government	Possible Opposition
1.	Ind, Prog, Com, SD	nil
2.	Ind, Prog, Com	SD
3.	Ind, Prog, SD	Com
4.	Prog, Com, SD	Ind
5.	Ind, Com, SD	Prog
6.	Ind, SD	Prog, Com
7.	Ind, Prog	SD, Com
8.	Ind, Com	Prog, SD

The election itself comes to a very partial arbitration of the question "Who governs?" Only seven of the fifteen otherwise conceivable governments have been eliminated, leaving eight possibilities. Each party is a member of at least five such possible governments, and no party belongs to all eight. The effective choice must therefore rest with party leaders as they are influenced by conflicts and compatibilities of program, ideology, or personality in the formation of coalitions. It is a choice *bounded* but left undecided by the election outcome. As it happens, government 6 (Independence-Social Democrat) was formed in 1963, but roughly similar outcomes have since World War II, also led to the formation of governments 3, 4, and 7.[17] Unless the process of government formation is understood by the electorate, this surely raises important difficulties for theories of electoral representation, for it is impossible to see how the citizen could draw useful associations between his voting decision and the eventual choice of a government.[18]

Parliaments that are fractionalized enough to produce

17. Nils Andrain,
18. See Downs, pp, 142–63 for a discussion of these difficulties. In Thomas Casstevens, "An Axiom About Voting," *American Political Science Review*, 62 (1968), 205–07, an attempt is made to show that (on a simplistic assumption about "winning" and a vitiating assumption about the probabilities of parties doing so) the voter should always just vote for his most preferred party.

these uncertainties[19] would seem especially prone to government instability, for at least two reasons. First, their numerical structures offer *wide opportunity for the destruction of governments*. With more than one party-elite in a government, it is possible to reach a vote of no confidence even without a breach of party discipline. And, as the number of essential partners increases, one might expect an actuarial increase in the frequency with which a particular decision alienates a member party, bringing a new election or a change of governments without one. Moreover, since only one of 2^{np-1} possible governments has been formed, it seems probable that member parties could, at some point, identify alternative partners with whom a more attractive government could be formed. These reasons are very roughly analogous to the structural relations outlined for partisan insurgency earlier, although their interconnections are less clear. A second reason points toward the likelihood that highly fractionalized parliaments are indices of intense political conflict. If this is so, then there will be a convergence of strong motives and wide opportunities for changes of government in such systems.

Unhappily, none of these conjectures can be mistaken for a theory. And, although coalition behavior has been the object of intensive study in recent years, research on the specific question of stability remains inconclusive. We do, however, have a useful exploration of several commonsense hypotheses in a recent study by Michael Taylor and V. M. Herman.[20] These authors considered 196 governments in 19 countries (those studied here, minus the U.S. and Switzerland, plus Japan) from the end of World War II up to 1969. They define "government stability" in calendar days elapsed

19. If parliamentary fractionalization reaches .5, there may be no single-party solution, and if it reaches .75, there cannot possibly be such a solution.

20. "Party Systems and Government Stability," *American Political Science Review,* 65 (1971), 28–37.

without a change of prime minister or party support.[21] Their study is an effort to treat variation in stability as a function of the parliamentary party system variables discussed here. The most straightforward of their results are these.

Independent Variable	Product-Moment Correlation with Government Stability
(1) Number of parliamentary parties (n_p)	—.39
(2) Fractionalization of parliamentary parties (F_p)	—.448
(3) Number of parties in government	—.307
(4) Proportion of seats held by anti-system parties	—.450

These results tend to confirm the intuitive expectations sketched out above, but they do not include the most plausible explanation turned up by the Taylor-Herman study. It is interesting that their effort to include ideological distances in the notion of fractionalization actually weakened its relationship to instability (to —.417.) But the related distinction between anti-system and pro-system parties nevertheless proved highly interesting (variable 4 above.) Their best explanation turns on the joint effect of "proportion anti-system" and the fractionalization of seats among the remaining parties. Using these two variables in a multiple regression estimate they find a fit of $R = .496$. Ironically, the estimate is improved slightly ($R = .506$) if right-wing anti-system seats are dropped, leaving only communist seats in the proportion anti-system. The apparent explanation for this account is that, if anti-system parties always refuse to support governments, the proportion of available votes required is increased (being $r/2(r-a)$ where r is the parliament's size and a is the size of the anti-system contingent). The effective decision rule for sustaining governments thus grows more

21. In this, they follow an earlier study, Jean Blondel, "Party Systems and Patterns of Government in Western Democracies," *Canadian Journal of Political Science, 1* (1968), 180–203.

restrictive with increases in anti-system representation (or communists) and is less easily met as remaining seats grow more fractionalized. This seems, at any rate, the most plausible conjecture.

Although this section is less developed analytically than its predecessor, its *tendence* is similar—to suggest complexity of interconnection. I will not attempt to draw all of these connections together here, but finish with the conjecture that this analysis concerns itself with only a few fragments of the immeasurably *more* complex pattern by which ruling groups, as they are sustained and replaced over time, leave their marks on publics and the policies by which they are governed.

APPENDIXES

PROPOSITIONAL SUMMARY
OF FINDINGS

Similarity Proposition One: Electoral systems tend to award more than proportionate shares of parliamentary seats to parties with large shares of the vote, and to award less than proportionate shares of seats to parties with smaller shares of the vote.

Similarity Proposition Two: Electoral systems almost always award more than a proportionate share of the seats to the party which polls the largest single share of the vote.

Similarity Proposition Three: Most single-party parliamentary majorities are "manufactured" by electoral systems.

Similarity Proposition Four: Electoral laws often limit the number of legislative parties by granting no seats to small parties, especially those which finish last in the popular voting.

Similarity Proposition Five: Electoral systems defractionalize parliamentary party systems.

Similarity Proposition Six: The effect of electoral laws upon the competitive positions of political parties in legislatures is marginal by comparison to the effect of election outcomes.

Similarity Proposition Seven: All of the properties associated with plurality formulae are also associated with the Australian majority formula.

Differential Proposition One: The relative advantage of strong elective parties over weak ones found in all electoral systems tends to be greater under plurality or majority formulae than under proportional representation formulae.

Differential Proposition Two: Plurality and majority formulae tend to give a greater advantage to first parties than do proportional representation formulae.

Provisional Differential Proposition Three: Plurality formulae cause two-party systems. (Rejected)

Differential Proposition Three: Plurality formulae are always associated with two-party competition except where strong local minority parties exist, and other formulae are associated with two-party competition only where minority elective parties are very weak.

Differential Proposition Four: Proportional representation formulae tend to allocate seats more proportionally than do majority and plurality formulae.

Differential Proposition Five: Plurality and majority formulae tend to deny representation to larger numbers of small parties than proportional representation formulae.

Differential Proposition Six: P.R. electoral systems tend to be associated with more fractionalized elective and parliamentary party systems than plurality and majority formulae.

Differential Proposition Seven: Minimal legislative majorities will tend to be larger in bodies elected under P.R. formulae, and smaller in bodies elected under plurality and majority formulae.

Differential Proposition Eight: Plurality and majority formulae tend to magnify changes in the popular support of parties when legislative seats are allocated, but P.R. systems generally have no such effect.

Differential Proposition Nine: By comparison to *highest average* formulae, *largest remainder* formulae tend to be associated with:

    a. greater fractionalization in elective party systems

b. greater fractionalization in parliamentary systems
c. a more proportional allocation of seats
d. larger numbers of elective parties contesting elections
e. larger numbers of parliamentary parties holding seats
f. slightly weaker first parties (elective)
g. slightly weaker first parties (legislative)
h. leading two parties which are together slightly weaker (elective)
i. leading two parties which are together slightly weaker (legislative)
j. slightly larger minimal parliamentary majorities (A)

Differential Proposition Ten: The proportionality with which legislative seats are allocated increases in relation to magnitude of electoral districts: the higher the magnitude, the greater the proportionality.

Differential Proposition Ten (Corollary): The average deviation between the vote and seat shares of the parties (I) varies in an inverse proportion of district magnitude (M): as magnitudes increase, average deviations decrease.

Differential Proposition Eleven: The positive relationship between proportionality and district magnitude is curvilinear: as district magnitudes are increased, proportionality increases at a decreasing rate.

Differential Proposition Eleven (Corollary): The negative relationship between average vote-seat deviations (I) and district magnitude (M) is curvilinear: as district magnitudes are increased, deviations between vote and seat shares decrease at a decreasing rate.

Differential Proposition Twelve: The fractionalization of party systems, both elective and legislative, varies positively with district magnitude: high magnitudes are associated with great fractionalization, and vice versa. But the relationship is curvilinear: fractionalization increases at a decreasing rate as magnitude increases.

Differential Proposition Thirteen: The magnitude of electoral district (M) is positively related to:

a. minimal parliamentary majorities (A) entailing larger numbers of legislative parties
b. larger numbers of elective parties (N_e)
c. larger numbers of legislative parties (N_p)
d. first parties which obtain smaller shares of the vote and and seats (P_e and P_p)
e. first parties which receive smaller bonuses of seats ($P_p - P_e$)
f. first two-party pairs which receive smaller shares of the vote and seats (W_e and W_p)
g. first two-party pairs which receive smaller bonuses of seats ($W_p - W_e$)

APPENDIX B

I. GLOSSARY OF ALGEBRAIC TERMS

1. National-Level Symbols

A: minimal number of parliamentary parties required to form a majority, assuming full willingness to enter coalitions

E: the average vote share (E_e) or seat share (E_p) change per party between any two consecutive elections

F: the fractionalization of any elective (F_e) or parliamentary party system (F_p)

I: the average deviation between the vote and seat shares of parties in any election, parties with fewer than 2% of the vote excluded

M: the mean magnitude of electoral districts for an entire electoral system

N: the number of parties, elective (N_e) or parliamentary (N_p)

P: the vote or seat share of the strongest single elective (P_e) or parliamentary (P_p) party

S: the national seat share of any one party, as decimal or % of total seats awarded

T: the national vote share of any one party, as decimal or % of total vote

V: the absolute number of votes cast in an election

W: the vote or seat share of the strongest *two* elective (W_e) or parliamentary (W_p) parties

2. District-Level Symbols

c: the "constant cost" of a legislative seat, defined by the condition $s = t$

m: the magnitude of any given electoral district, viz., the number of seats it contains

q: an "electoral quota" as defined by formula given

s: the seat share of any one party, as decimal or % of total district seats awarded

t: the vote share of any one party, as decimal or % of district vote polled

v: the absolute number of votes cast in any one electoral district

3. Subscripts

e: subscript which denotes any quantity pertaining to elective party competition

p: subscript which denotes a quantity pertaining to parliamentary or legislative party competition

(a, b, c, d . . . n):   subscript sequence denoting quantities pertaining to individual parties, from strongest (a) to weakest (n), either in votes or seats as shown in other terms of formulae

LIST OF ELECTIONS ANALYZED

NATION	DATE	DATA AVAILABLE
1. Australia	September 1946	all
2. "	December 1949	all
3. "	April 1951	all
4. "	May 1954	all
5. "	December 1955	seats complete; votes partial
6. "	November 1958	all
7. "	December 1961	all
8. "	November 1963	all
9. Austria	November 1945	seats complete; votes partial
10. "	October 1949	all, except minor elective parties
11. "	February 1953	all
12. "	May 1956	all
13. "	May 1959	all
14. "	November 1962	all
15. Belgium	February 1946	all
16. "	June 1949	all
17. "	June 1950	all
18. "	April 1954	all
19. "	June 1958	all
20. "	March 1961	all

21.	Canada	June 1945	all
22.	"	June 1949	all
23.	"	August 1953	all
24.	"	June 1957	all
25.	"	March 1958	all
26.	"	June 1962	all
27.	"	April 1963	all
28.	Denmark	October 1945	all
29.	"	October 1947	all
30.	"	September 1950	all
31.	"	April 1953	all
32.	"	September 1953	all
33.	"	May 1957	all
34.	"	November 1960	all
35.	"	September 1964	all
36.	Finland	March 1945	all
37.	"	July 1948	all
38.	"	July 1951	all
39.	"	March 1954	all
40.	"	July 1958	all
41.	"	February 1962	all
42.	France	October 1945	all
43.	"	June 1946	all
44.	"	July 1951	all
45.	"	January 1956	all
46.	"	November 1958	all
47.	"	November 1962	all
48.	West Germany	August 1949	all
49.	"	September 1953	all
50.	"	September 1957	all
51.	"	October 1961	all
52.	Great Britain	July 1945	all
53.	"	February 1950	all
54.	"	October 1951	all
55.	"	May 1955	all
56.	"	October 1959	all
57.	"	October 1964	all
58.	Iceland	June 1946	all
59.	"	October 1949	all

60. Iceland	June 1953	all
61. "	June 1956	all
62. "	June 1959	all
63. "	October 1959	all
64. "	June 1963	all
65. Ireland (Eire)	February 1948	all
66. "	May 1951	all
67. "	May 1954	all
68. "	March 1957	all
69. "	October 1961	all
70. Israel	January 1949	all
71. "	July 1951	all
72. "	July 1955	all
73. "	November 1959	all
74. "	August 1961	all
75. Italy	June 1946	all
76. "	April 1948	all
77. "	June 1953	all
78. "	May 1958	all
79. "	April 1963	all
80. Luxembourg	May 1954	all
81. "	February 1959	all
82. "	June 1964	all
83. Netherlands	May 1946	all
84. "	July 1948	all
85. "	June 1952	all
86. "	June 1956	all
87. "	June 1959	all
88. "	May 1963	all
89. New Zealand	November 1946	all
90. "	November 1949	all
91. "	September 1951	all
92. "	November 1954	all
93. "	November 1957	all
94. "	November 1960	all
95. "	November 1963	all
96. Norway	October 1945	all
97. "	October 1947	all
98. "	October 1953	all

99. Norway	October 1957	all
100. "	September 1961	all
101. Sweden	September 1948	all
102. "	September 1952	all
103. "	September 1956	all
104. "	June 1958	all
105. "	September 1960	all
106. "	September 1964	all
107. Switzerland	October 1947	all
108. "	October 1951	seats only
109. "	October 1955	seats only
110. "	October 1959	seats only
111. "	October 1963	seats only
112. United States	November 1946	all
113. "	November 1948	all
114. "	November 1950	all
115. "	November 1952	all
116. "	November 1954	all
117. "	November 1956	all
118. "	November 1958	all
119. "	November 1960	all
120. "	November 1962	all
121. "	November 1964	all

ELECTORAL LAW SOURCES

AUSTRALIA:
Leslie F. Crisp, *The Parliamentary Government of the Common-wealth of Australia* (3d ed. London, Longmans, 1961) Joan Rydon, "Electoral Methods and the Australian Party System: 1910–1951," *The Australian Journal of Politics and History, 2* (Nov. 1956), 68–83; Geoffrey Sawyer, *Australian Government Today* (rev., Parksville, Melbourne University Press, 1961).

AUSTRIA:
"Austria in 1959," *World Today, 15* (Aug. 1959), 441–50; Wolfgang Birke, *European Elections by Direct Suffrage* (Leyden, A. W. Sythoff, 1961); Peter Berger, "Elections and Parties in Austria," *Journal of Politics, 12* (Aug. 1950), 511–29; Kurt L. Shell, *The Transformation of Austrian Socialism* (New York, State University of New York, 1962).

BELGIUM:
"Belgian Parliament Chosen by List P.R.," *National Municipal Review, 43* (May 1954), 253–54; George van den Bergh, *Unity in Diversity: A Systematic Critical Analysis of All Electoral Systems* (London, B. T. Batsford, 1956), p. 16; Wolfgang Birke, *European Elections by Direct Suffrage*, pp. 34–36; Jeffrey Obler, "Political Parties and Leadership Recruitment in Belgium" (unpublished M.A. thesis, University of Wisconsin, 1965), pp. 55–69; John G. Grumm, "Theories of Electoral Systems," *Midwest Journal of Political Science, 2* (Nov. 1958), 357–76.

CANADA:
Canada Year Book, 1965 (Ottawa, Minister of Trade and Commerce, 1965), pp. 69–75.

DENMARK:
Nils Andrèn, *Government and Politics in the Nordic Countries* (Stockholm, Almquist and Wiksell, 1964), pp. 40–42, 226–27; Wolfgang Birke, *European Elections by Direct Suffrage*, pp. 37–40; John G. Grumm, "Theories of Electoral Systems," *Midwest Journal of Political Science*, 2 (Nov. 1958), 357–76; Enid Lakeman and James D. Lambert, *Voting in Democracies* (London, Faber and Faber, 1955), pp. 172–77; "New Danish Constitution in Effect," *National Municipal Review, 42* (Sept. 1953).

FINLAND:
Nils Andrèn, *Government and Politics in the Nordic Countries*, pp. 70–72; Eric C. Bellquist, "Finland: Democracy in Travail," *Western Political Quarterly*, 2 (1949), 217–27; Arvid Enckell, *Democratic Finland* (London, Herbert Joseph, 1949), pp. 32, 33, 121; "Finland Holds Democratic Elections," *National Municipal Review, 34* (May 1945), pp. 251–52.

FRANCE:
Peter Campbell, *French Electoral Systems and Elections Since 1789* (London, Faber and Faber, 1958), 134–35; *Les Élections de 2 Janvier, 1956*, ed. Maurice Duverger, Francois Goguel, and Jean Touchand (Paris, Armand Colm, 1956), 472–505.

GERMANY:
Facts About Germany, 4th ed. (Press and Information Office, Federal German Government, Bonn, 1962), pp. 81–85; Uwe W. Kitzenger, *German Electoral Politics* (London, Oxford University Press, 1960), pp. 17–37; James K. Pollock, "The West German Electoral Law of 1953," *American Political Science Review*, 49 (Mar. 1955), 107–30.

ICELAND:
Nils Andrèn, *Government and Politics in the Nordic Countries*, pp. 99–101; *Hagskyrslur Islands* II, 24 (Reykjavik, Statistical Bureau of Iceland, 1960).

IRELAND:
Wolfgang Birke, *European Elections by Direct Suffrage*, pp. 43–44; *Elections Abroad*, ed. David E. Butler (London, Macmillan and Co., Ltd., 1959), pp. 183–85, 223–25; J. F. S. Ross, *The Irish Election System* (London, Pall Mall Press, 1959), p. 95; *Statistical*

Abstract of Ireland, 1959 (Dublin, The Central Stationery Office, 1959), p. 59.

ISRAEL:

Benjamin Akzin, "The Role of Parties in Israeli Democracy," *Journal of Politics*, *17* (Nov. 1955), 507-45; Arye Arazi, *Le Système Electoral Israélien* (Geneva, Librarie Droz, 1963), pp. 20-38; "Israel Changes P.R. Rules; Holds New Elections," *National Municipal Review*, *40* (Sept. 1951), 433-34; "Israel Constituent Assembly Elected by P.R.," *National Municipal Review*, *38* (Mar. 1949), 144-45.

ITALY:

Wolfgang Birke, *European Elections by Direct Suffrage*, pp. 44-46; "Italy's General Election," *World Today*, *9* (July 1953), 277-79; "Italy Takes Steps to Return to P.R.," *National Municipal Review*, *43* (July 1954), 367; David S. McLellan and Robert McLellan, "The 1963 Italian Elections," *Western Political Quarterly*, *17* (Dec. 1964), 671-89; "P.R. Elections in Many Lands," *National Municipal Review*, *35* (July 1946), 371-74; "P.R. Election Gives Italy First One-Party Majority," *National Municipal Review*, *37* (June 1948), 335-37.

LUXEMBOURG:

Wolfgang Birke, *European Elections by Direct Suffrage*, pp. 46-47; *Bulletin de Documentation*, Grand Duché de Luxembourg, Ministère d'État, *7* (June 30, 1951); *Bulletin de Documentation*, Grand Duché de Luxembourg, Ministère d'État, *15* (Feb.-Mar. 1959); *Bulletin de Documentation*, Grand Duché de Luxembourg, Ministère d'État, *20* (July 23, 1964); Ruth Putnam, "The Luxembourg Chamber of Deputies," *American Political Science Review*, *14* (Aug. 1920), 607-34; *The Grand Duchy of Luxembourg* (Washington, D.C., mimeographed outline, Embassy of Luxembourg, 1966); unpublished memo from Information Desk, U.S. Embassy of Luxembourg, to the author, May 25, 1966.

NETHERLANDS:

George van den Bergh, *Unity in Diversity: A Systematic Critical Analysis of All Electoral Systems*, pp. 16, 30-32, 36, 38; Robert C. Bone, "The Dynamics of Dutch Politics," *Journal of Politics*, *24* (Feb. 1962), 30; J. A. LaPonce, "The Protection of Minorities by the Electoral System," *Western Political Quarterly*, *10* (June 1957), 334.

NEW ZEALAND:

R. M. Chapman, W. K. Jackson, A. V. Mitchell, *New Zealand*

Politics in Action: The 1960 General Election (London, Oxford University Press, 1962), pp. 37, 1124; *New Zealand Official Year Book, 1961* (Wellington, Government Printer, 1961), pp. 3–12.

NORWAY:

Nils Andrèn, *Government and Politics in the Nordic Countries,* pp. 121–23; James A. Storing, *Norwegian Democracy* (Boston, Houghton Mifflin, 1963), pp. 61–72; James A. Storing, "Unique Features of the Norwegian Storting," *Western Political Quarterly, 16* (Mar. 1963), 161.

SWEDEN:

Nils Andrèn, *Government and Politics in the Nordic Countries,* pp. 182–83, 232–33; Nils Herlitz, "Proportional Representation in Sweden," *American Political Science Review, 19* (Aug. 1925), 582–92; Richard C. Spencer, "Party Government and the Swedish Riksdag," *American Political Science Review, 39* (June 1945), 437–58; "Sweden Holds National Elections," *National Municipal Review, 37* (Nov. 1948), 557–58.

SWITZERLAND

Christopher Hughes, *The Parliament of Switzerland* (London, Cassell and Co., 1962), pp. 37–51; "Switzerland Chooses Lower House by List System," *National Municipal Review, 41* (Feb. 1952), 108.

SOME DISTRICT PAYOFF FUNCTIONS

Here are some analytic results describing the proportions of a district vote which can (or must) win a given number of seats for a particular party. They are derived from a collaborative effort involving John Loosemore, Vic Hanby, and myself at the University of Essex, England, during the spring term of 1970.

We consider three variables: n parties in the district, contesting m seats, and winning s of these (s = 0, 1, 2, ... m). We define two thresholds for a party's proportion of the district vote: (1.) the minimum number of votes that could possibly win s or more seats, and (2.) the maximum proportion of the vote that could fail to win at least s of m seats. These are what we mean by the "threshold of representation" and the "threshold of exclusion." All are for electoral formulae as defined in Chapter 2 except for the St. Lague formulae, where we have (inaccurately) used the numerical series 1, 3, 5, ... (2m − 1) instead of the series 1.4, 3.5, ... (2m − 1). The functions are these:

	THRESHOLD OF REPRESENTATION	THRESHOLD OF EXCLUSION
d'Hondt	$\dfrac{s}{m+n-1}$	$\dfrac{s}{m+1}$
St. Lague	$\dfrac{2s-1}{2m+n-2}$	$\dfrac{2s-1}{2m}$
L-Rem	$\dfrac{s-1}{m} + \dfrac{1}{mn}$	$\dfrac{2s-1}{2m}$

This approach is inspired by Stein Rokkan's very useful "Elections: Electoral Systems," in *International Encyclopedia of the Social Sciences* (New York: Crowell-Collier-Macmillan, 1968).

APPENDIX F

FRACTIONALIZATION BY COUNTRY

MEAN FRACTIONALIZATION 1945-65

NATION	MEAN ELECTORAL FRACTION-ALIZATION (F_e)	MEAN LEGISLATIVE FRACTION-ALIZATION (F_p)
1. U.S.A.	0.50	0.48
2. New Zealand	0.54	0.49
3. Australia	0.56	0.49
4. Great Britain	0.58	0.52
5. Austria	0.61	0.56
6. Canada	0.66	0.52
7. Belgium	0.67	0.62
8. Luxembourgh	0.70	0.66
9. Ireland	0.70	0.67
10. Sweden	0.70	0.68
11. Norway	0.73	0.67
12. West Germany	0.73	0.69
13. Iceland	0.73	0.70
14. Italy	0.74	0.71
15. Denmark	0.75	0.74
16. Netherlands	0.78	0.77
17. France	0.81	0.77
18. Finland	0.81	0.78
19. Switzerland	0.81	0.79
20. Israel	0.81	0.80

Note: These data first appeared as "A Note on the Fractionalization of Some European Party Systems," *Comparative Political Studies*, 1 (1968), 413-18.

SELECTED BIBLIOGRAPHY

BOOKS

Andrèn, Nils, *Government and Politics in the Nordic Countries*, Stockholm, Almquist and Wiksell, 1964.

Arazi, Arye, *Le Système Electoral Israélien*, Geneva, Librarie Droz, 1963.

Bagehot, Walter, *The English Constitution*, New York, D. Appleton, 1877.

Birke, Wolfgang, *European Elections by Direct Suffrage*, Leyden, A. W. Sythoff, 1961.

Butler, David E., *The Electoral System in Britain Since 1918*, Oxford, Oxford University Press, 1963.

Campbell, Peter, *French Electoral Systems and Elections Since 1789*, London, Faber and Faber, 1958.

Chapman, R. M., W. K. Jackson, and A. V. Mitchell, *New Zealand Politics in Action: The 1960 General Election*, London, Oxford University Press.

Duverger, Maurice, *Political Parties*, translated by Barbara and Robert North, New York, John Wiley and Sons, 1954.

Duverger, Maurice, *L'Influence des Systèmes Electoraux sur la Vie Politique*, Paris, Armand Colin, 1954.

Elections Abroad, ed. David E. Butler, London, Macmillan, 1959.

Les Elections de 2 Janvier, 1956, eds. Maurice Duverger, François Goguel, and Jean Touchand, Paris, Armand Colin, 1956.

Essays on the Behavioral Study of Politics, ed. Austin Ranney, chapter on "The Utility and Limitations of Aggregate Data in the Study of Electoral Behavior," by Austin Ranney, Urbana, University of Illinois Press, 1962.

Essays in Political Science, ed. Edward H. Buehrig, chapter on "Political Parties in Western Democratic Systems," by Leon Epstein, Bloomington, Indiana University Press, 1966.

Friedrich, Carl J., *Constitutional Government and Democracy*, Boston, Ginn and Co., 1950.

Hogan, James, *Elections and Representation*, University College, Cork, Cork University Press, 1945.

Hughes, Christopher, *The Parliament of Switzerland*, London, Cassell and Co., 1962.

Key, V. O., Jr., *Politics, Parties and Pressure Groups*, 5th ed., New York, Thomas Y. Crowell, 1952.

Kitzinger, Uwe W., *German Electoral Politics*, London, Oxford University Press, 1960.

Lakeman, Enid, and James D. Lambert, *Voting in Democracies*, London, Faber and Faber, 1955.

Lane, Robert E., *Political Life*, New York, The Free Press, 1959.

Lipset, Seymour Martin, *Political Man: The Social Bases of Politics*, Garden City, N.Y., Doubleday, 1959.

Mackenzie, William J. M., *Free Elections: An Elementary Textbook*, New York, Rinehart and Co., 1958.

Macridis, Roy C., *The Study of Comparative Government*, Garden City, N.Y., Doubleday, 1945.

Mill, John Stuart, *Considerations on Representative Government*, London, Longmans, Green, 1890.

Modern Political Parties, ed. Sigmund Neumann, Chicago, University of Chicago Press, 1956.

Modern Political Systems—Europe, ed. Roy C. Macridis and Robert E. Ward, Englewood Cliffs, N.J., Prentice-Hall, 1963.

Political Handbook and Atlas of the World, ed. Walter H. Mallory, 18th–38th eds. New York, Harper and Row, 1945–1965.

Political Oppositions in Western Democracies, ed. Robert A. Dahl, New Haven, Yale University Press, 1966.

Politics and Social Life, eds. Nelson W. Polsby, Robert A. Dentler, and Paul A. Smith, chapter on "An Illustrative Axiomatic System," by David Braybrooke, Boston, Houghton Mifflin, 1963.

Ross, J. F. S., *The Irish Election System*, London, Pall Mall Press, 1959.

Sartori, Giovanni, *Democratic Theory*, New York, Frederick A. Praeger, 1965.

Sawyer, Geoffrey, *Australian Government Today*, rev. ed. Parksville, Melbourne University Press, 1961.

Scarrow, Harold A., *Canada Votes*, New Orleans, Hauser Press, 1962.

Schattschneider, E. E., *Party Government*, New York, Holt, Rinehart and Winston, 1942.

Shell, Kurt L., *The Transformation of Australian Socialism*, New York, State University of New York, 1962.

Storing, James A., *Norwegian Democracy*, Boston, Houghton Mifflin, 1963.

Svalastoga, Kaare, *Social Differentiation*, New York, David McKay, 1965.

Thorson, Thomas Landon, *The Logic of Democracy*, New York, Holt, Rinehart and Winston, 1962.

van den Bergh, George, *Unity in Diversity: A Systematic Critical Analysis of All Electoral Systems*, London, B. T. Batsford, 1956.

ARTICLES

Abraham, Henry J., "One Way to Get Out the Vote," *National Municipal Review, 39* (Sept. 1950), 395–99.

Akzin, Benjamin, "The Role of Parties in Israeli Democracy," *Journal of Politics, 17* (Nov. 1955), 507–45.

Andrews, William G., "The By-Election System of the Fifth French Republic," *Western Political Quarterly, 17* (Dec. 1964), 690–702.

Bellquist, Eric C., "Finland: Democracy in Travail," *Western Political Quarterly, 2* (1949), 217–27.

Berger, Peter, "Elections and Parties in Austria," *Journal of Politics, 12* (Aug. 1950), 511–29.

Bone, Robert C., "The Dynamics of Dutch Politics," *Journal of Politics, 24* (Feb. 1962), 23–49.

Dami, A., "In Support of Proportional Representation," *International Social Science Bulletin, 3* (Summer 1951), 353–57.

Duverger, Maurice, "The Influence of Electoral Systems on Political Life," *International Social Science Bulletin, 3* (Summer 1951), 314–52.

Elder, Neil, "Parliamentary Government in Scandinavia," *Parliamentary Affairs* (Summer 1960), pp. 363–73.

Grumm, John G., "Theories of Electoral Systems," *Midwest Journal of Political Science, 2* (Nov. 1958), 357–76.

Herlitz, Nils, "Proportional Representation in Sweden," *American Political Science Review, 19* (Aug. 1925), 582–92.

Kendall, M. G., and A. Stuart, "Cubic Proportion in Electoral Results," *British Journal of Sociology, 1* (1950), 183 ff.

Kircheimer, Otto, "Majorities and Minorities in Western European Governments," *Western Political Quarterly, 12* (June 1959), 492–510.

LaPonce, J. A., "The Protection of Minorities by the Electoral System," *Western Political Quarterly, 10* (June 1957), 318–39.

Lipson, Leslie, "The Two-Party System in British Politics," *American Political Science Review, 47* (June 1953), 337–58.

March, James G., "Party Legislative Representation as a Function of Election Results," *Public Opinion Quarterly, 21* (Winter 1957–58), 521–42.

McLellan, David S., and Robert McLellan, "The 1963 Italian Elections," *Western Political Quarterly, 17* (Dec. 1964), 671–89.

Noonan, Lowell G., "The Decline of the British Liberal Party," *Journal of Politics, 16* (Feb. 1954), 24–38.

Pollock, James K., "The West German Electoral Law of 1953," *American Political Science Review, 49* (Mar. 1955), 107–30.

Putnam, Ruth, "The Luxembourg Chamber of Deputies," *American Political Science Review, 14* (Aug. 1920), 607–34.

Rokkan, Stein, "Electoral Systems," draft article for International Encyclopedia of Social Science.

Rustow, Dankwart A., "Some Observations on Proportional Representation," *Journal of Politics, 12* (Feb. 1950), 107–22.

Rydon, Joan, "Electoral Methods and the Australian Party System: 1910–1951," *The Australian Journal of Politics and History, 12* (Nov. 1956), 68–83.

Scarrow, Harold A., "Vote Turnout in Canada," *Midwest Journal of Political Science, 5* (1961), 351–64.

Silva, Ruth C., "Compared Values of the Single and the Multi-Member Legislative District," *Western Political Quarterly, 17* (Sept. 1964), 504–16.

Storing, James A., "Unique Features of the Norwegian Storting," *Western Political Quarterly, 16* (March 1963), 161–66.

Wildavsky, Aaron B., "A Methodological Critique of Duverger's *Political Parties*," *Journal of Politics, 21* (May 1959), 303–18.

DOCUMENTS

Canada Year Book, 1965, Ottawa, Minister of Trade and Commerce, 1965.

Grand Duché de Luxembourg, Ministère d'Etat, *Bulletin de Documentation*, 7 (June 30, 1951).

Grand Duché de Luxembourg, Ministère d'Etat, *Bulletin de Documentation*, 15 (Feb.–Mar. 1959).

Grand Duché de Luxembourg, Ministère d'Etat, *Bulletin de Documentation*, 20 (July 23, 1964).

The Grand Duchy of Luxembourg, Washington, D.C., Embassy of Luxembourg, 1966.

Hagskyrslur Islands, Vol. II, No. 24, Reykjavik, Statistical Bureau of Iceland, 1960.

Keesing's Contemporary Archives, 5–14 (1943–64), London, Keesing's Publication.

New Zealand Official Yearbook, 1961, 66th issue, Wellington: Government Printer, 1961.

Ninth Census of Canada, 1 (1951). Ottawa, Ministry of Trade and Commerce, 1953.

Official Yearbook of the Commonwealth of Australia, No. 51 (1965), Camberra, Commonwealth Bureau of Statistics, 1965.

Statistical Abstract of Ireland, 1959, Dublin, The Central Stationery Office, 1959.

INDEX